Cathedrals and Cappuccinos

A notebook of journeys to England's 42 Anglican Cathedrals

Trish Rogers

Published in 2013 by Naturalbridge Books

4, Penifiler, Portree, Isle of Skye. IV51 9NF

For further information email: pmrdhr@hotmail.com

Produced by Strath Print, Broadford, Isle of Skye

Typeset – Palatino Roman

Front cover:
Heptatych with images of the first 27 cathedrals: Birmingham – Lichfield.

Back cover:
Pentatych with images of the last 15 cathedrals: Guildford – Newcastle.

A catalogue record for this book is available from the British Library

ISBN 978-0-9545381-3-2

125

Acknowledgements

Firstly I would like to pay tribute to the cathedrals themselves and the superb people who sustain their life and upkeep. Cathedrals are part of our national heritage but have no guaranteed funding from the government.

I am extremely grateful to all the people who gave me encouragement and help in producing this book, especially:

Brenda Hilton, who gave me a master class in grammar and punctuation

Chris Wood, who helped me formulate the Introduction and Reflections

Ed King, who proof read and commented on the entire text

Peter Fox, who gave advice on the design

Friends on Skye for support and good advice

The Bumnotes for their constructive criticism

Many thanks to those who joined me on various stages of my cathedral journey. They are noted at the top of the relevant cathedral entry. They were as follows:

Dave Rogers, my late husband and dearest companion

Les Hilton, retired Maths teacher and Dave's colleague, and his wife Brenda, friends from our former life in Sutton Coldfield

Viv Yates, who had been our Russian teacher at the Brasshouse Centre, Birmingham

Wendy Ashwood, Ann & Mike Scorer and Claire Barnham, friends from the Bumnotes, a group connected with university days

Peter Fox, my elder brother and Joy his wife

Michael Porteus, a previous Rector of St. Columba's Episcopal Church, Portree, Skye, before moving to Cornwall

Enid Faulkner, the friend who introduced me to the Skye Quaker meeting. She moved to Northamptonshire in 2006

Rick Jones, my colleague from the West Midlands Probation Service.

Thanks too to all those who showed an interest in my original project, particularly my brother, Philip Fox, and his wife, Shena, who gave me the book 'Discovering Cathedrals' by David Peplow.

Thanks also to Strath Print for their time and attention in preparing this for printing, and for producing the final book.

Foreword

The cathedrals of England are among the country's greatest glories. Sermons in stone, they represent an unparalleled history of architecture and design through a thousand years, their construction itself a matter for wonder, speculation and profound admiration of the creativity, innovation and labour that accomplished them. But this built heritage encompasses far more than just construction. Cathedrals have been, and remain today, centres of great art and music, education, pastoral care and social responsibility. To wander through them, in all their diversity, is to become vividly aware of the history of a whole region, and indeed of a whole country.

In joining the great stream of pilgrims who have visited English cathedrals, Trish Rogers brings her own impressions, interests and sensibilities before our eyes and invites us to join her on a journey that few of us will ever have the time or opportunity to enjoy. Nor does she neglect the bodily wellbeing of the pilgrim – in the past, cathedrals fed the poor in their refectories and kitchens, and an aspect of this task still remains in the cafes that are almost invariably a well-frequented part of cathedral life today (though the cappuccinos are a very 21st century introduction, the religious derivation of the name notwithstanding).

But above all, cathedrals are, as they have been since the beginning, spiritual communities. The rich culture and history of each one is the expression of people from every background and walk of life gathering around, not just a building but a story, a calling, an invitation to discipleship and community, and the rhythms of a faith-filled life. At the heart of every cathedral is the practice of daily prayer and praise, of witness and mission and service. These cathedrals are not museums of the past but living testimonies to the gospel of Jesus Christ in the present.

Trish Rogers is offering royalties from her book to Christian Aid, for whom she previously worked as a volunteer. Christian Aid is also a spiritual community, bringing churches and supporters in the UK and Ireland close to partners in places of great poverty across the world, in service and prayer. The spiritual community of Christian Aid is in a different way a living testimony to the good news of Jesus Christ, and it is in that spirit of community that I commend Cathedrals and Cappuccinos to you. May you be blessed in the reading of it.

Kathy Galloway, Head of Christian Aid Scotland

Contents

Introduction

'Cathedrals and Cappuccinos' follows the journeys I took to explore each of the Anglican cathedrals in England. Virtually everyone has visited a cathedral at some time and most people probably have a favourite. Visiting all the cathedrals can bring many surprises and delights, some of which I hope will be discovered in these pages.

The book consists of snapshots, sketches and a series of impressions to whet the appetite rather than to attempt a comprehensive description of each cathedral. In addition to photographs I have included some of my artwork. Sketching and painting different aspects of a cathedral can be a way of gaining a greater appreciation of their amazing design and craftsmanship. The richness of cathedral art, culture and history is unsurpassed, an expression of their prime function as spiritual communities.

'Cappuccino' is included in the title of the book, since taking refreshments in the cathedral refectories, or cafés, became an important part of the experience. I have been told that Cappuccino also has tentative religious connotations, taking its name from the colour of the 16th century Capuchin monk's habit.

So what set me off on this fascinating journey?

Shortly before my sixtieth birthday, I made a list of the things I would like to do by way of celebration. One of the most ambitious ideas was a project to visit all the cathedrals in England.

When I first had this thought, I had no idea what it would involve. I imagined it would simply mean visiting 'medieval' cathedrals (those built before the Reformation) and that it would be completed during my 60th year. However, a book called 'Discovering Cathedrals' by David Pepin – an early birthday present – challenged those assumptions. Furthermore, the book was so useful that it subsequently became my main reference point. The first thing I learnt from it was the definition of a cathedral: "A cathedral is the main church in a church district known as a diocese (in this case Anglican or Church of England) where the bishop of the diocese has his cathedra or throne". The second was that, in England, there were 42 dioceses, or church districts, which covered every part of the country. The significance of this only began to dawn on us when we started planning our journeys.

My motivation for the project was a mixture of nostalgia and subterfuge.

The nostalgia was for the 1950s and '60s when I occasionally visited cathedrals with my family when on holiday. I began collecting a series of booklets called the Pitkin Cathedral Guides. Forty or so years later, I found them gathering dust on my bookshelf. They were a pleasant reminder of those visits during my teenage years and, particularly, of the time spent fathoming out the different styles of cathedral architecture with my father. I'd often wanted to look further into the subject, but had never had the opportunity.

The subterfuge involved Dave, my husband. He was an avid bird-watcher and had always preferred to escape to the countryside at holiday time. In fact, buildings didn't interest him and cities gave him claustrophobia. I was happy enough in the countryside, but I also wanted us to see something of our cultural heritage. It occurred to me that the cathedral project might entice Dave into a few cities. He might even appreciate something of the magnificence of these buildings. I knew my plan had worked in part when, some months into the project, I overheard him talking animatedly to friends about our visits ... he had seen a peregrine falcon on Lincoln Cathedral.

We gradually realised that this was going to be a major undertaking, not made any easier by the fact that, living on Skye, we would have to travel 300 miles or so before we even reached the English border. Each journey was, therefore, planned to incorporate special events, visits to family and friends and, of course, an RSPB Reserve or two. In all it took just over five years and thirteen journeys to complete.

Dave was my long suffering companion and chauffeur for about half of the visits, until his untimely death in November 2010. We developed quite a civilised approach to our tour of each cathedral. We would buy a Guidebook and then adjourn to the Refectory to study it over a cappuccino (and perhaps a slice of carrot cake). Then, suitably refreshed and with a slightly better knowledge of its features, we would enter the cathedral and stand at the west end, looking down the Nave to get a sense of the atmosphere of the place. After this we would probably go our separate ways to view the rest of the building. When we met at the end, I would invariably find that Dave had spotted all sorts of interesting features that I'd totally missed. He was naturally much more observant than me.

Alongside the Guidebooks, I collected the same memento from each cathedral – a pencil with a rubber. Dave, on the other hand (himself an organist) bought CDs of the cathedrals' famous organists, to play on our journeys.

It was always more interesting to visit a cathedral with someone else and I was fortunate to be accompanied by friends or relatives (namely the people I was staying with) to all but six of the cathedrals. I have listed these companions in the Acknowledgements and indicated which cathedral they visited with me.

Finally, I suppose the word 'misericord' (those tiny carved ledges, hidden under medieval choir seats and designed to offer support to aging monks through long periods of worship), could also have featured in the title, since I refer to them constantly. They are my passion. I'm not sure when I first encountered them, but I must have discovered them in those teenage years on holiday with my parents. I love their exquisite, delicate carvings, and their lively, interesting subjects. I love the fact that they would have been hidden, like a guilty secret, under the seat of an aging monk. I love the glimpse they, literally, give into the ups and downs of the history of cathedrals. If you were looking for just one captivating feature in a cathedral, you could do worse than seek out misericords.

So I invite you to join me on this journey and perhaps make one of your own. Enjoy the distinctive spirituality, heritage, richness and history of each cathedral. Explore its effect on you and how it speaks to your spirituality and that of the present age. Feast on the misericords, gaze upward, let your spirits be lifted and enriched. And have a cappuccino!

1. Birmingham
2. Gloucester
3. Bristol
4. Durham
5. Ripon
6. York
7. Lincoln
8. Peterborough
9. Ely
10. Norwich
11. St Edmundsbury
12. Wells
13. Exeter
14. Worcester
15. Carlisle
16. St. Albans
17. Canterbury
18. Southwark
19. London St Pauls
20. Salisbury
21. Winchester
22. Portsmouth
23. Chichester
24. Coventry
25. Rochester
26. Hereford
27. Lichfield
28. Guildford
29. Truro
30. Chelmsford
31. Derby
32. Oxford
33. Blackburn
34. Bradford
35. Manchester
36. Wakefield
37. Sheffield
38. Southwell
39. Leicester
40. Chester
41. Liverpool
42. Newcastle

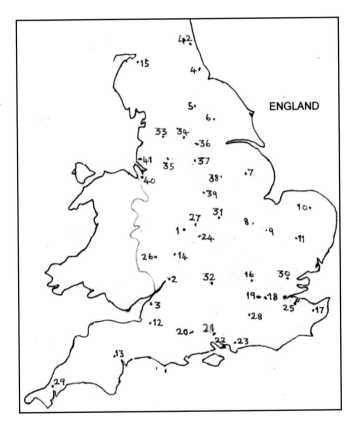

Map of the Cathedrals

Plan of a cathedral

North

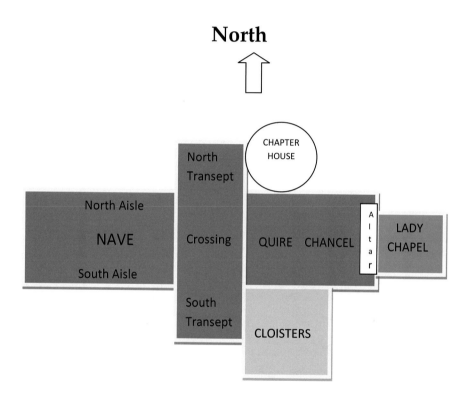

The First Three

Detail from the Nativity window
BIRMINGHAM CATHEDRAL

Birmingham Cathedral

23rd February 2007   *with Dave, Les & Brenda*

The start of my cathedral pilgrimage was rather a surprise. My initial thought had been to visit only 'medieval' cathedrals – those which had been built before the Reformation – which I had considered the true representation of what a cathedral was.

My plans were waylaid by Les and Brenda, enthusiastic friends who had entered into the spirit of the enterprise before I had really thought it through. They had spotted a lunchtime concert at Birmingham Cathedral and felt this would be the perfect way to start my epic project. They, therefore, whisked Dave, my husband, and me off to this 'Music for Lunch' concert. Soup and cups of tea were provided by the cathedral and we took these into the back row to consume with our sandwiches, while we listened to the concert.

The programme was a recital by Abigail Bennett, a soprano, who had been a chorister at both Wells and Birmingham Cathedrals and was now studying German and Music at Birmingham University. She sang pieces by Vivaldi, Mozart, Purcell, Bach, Schubert and Madeline Dring. My favourite was Schubert's "Die Forelle".

At the end of the concert I looked round the cathedral. Our visit had been so unexpected that I didn't have a real plan of how to assess the experience. Les and Brenda bought me a guide and ceremoniously signed it, "May this be the first of your cathedrals in this special six months of your life".

A brief survey of the relatively simple 'English Baroque' interior revealed an elegance and compactness. The balconies either side of the Nave made it resemble a non conformist building more than a cathedral. There was no vaulted Nave, ornately carved Quire, Lady Chapel or Cloisters. The most dominant features were the four Burne-Jones windows with their dramatic red stained glass: three behind, and either side of, the Altar representing the Nativity, Ascension and Crucifixion and one, at the west end of the Nave, representing the Last Judgement. During the war they were removed and stored down a mineshaft in Wales, thus avoiding the bomb which set the cathedral ablaze on 7 November 1940.

1998 was the last time I had entered this unlikely cathedral, which stands in a tiny oasis of green in the centre of this busy, multicultural city. It was during the time of the 'Jubilee 2000' Third World Debt Campaign, when a 70,000 strong 'Human Chain' surrounded Birmingham and world leaders at the G8 Conference.

Gloucester Cathedral

25th February 2007   *with Dave*

For years we had passed Gloucester Cathedral on the M5, on our way to visit Dave's family, viewing it in the distance, its tower rising elegantly above the cityscape. So, on this Sunday afternoon, we decided to take a detour and go as pilgrims to worship at this one-time abbey and monastery, and explore its treasures.

Peace pervaded its precincts. The Nave with its vast vaulted ceiling displayed a majestic simplicity. Immediately my heart felt in tune with the angelic strains from the rehearsing choir.

In due course we were led into the Quire and seated in the ancient choir stalls with their secret carved misericords. We prepared for evensong. In contrast to the Nave, we were surrounded by ornate furnishings. Stained glass windows rose like transparent walls enriching the light with glorious colours. Stories were carved into the wood and stone, decorating the screen, pulpit, lectern and pew ends.

The service began with plainsong chants as old as the cathedral stones – simple liturgy, sublime song. Readings on repentance from Jonah and Luke and a short talk for Lent followed.

And then the anthem. The choir processed silently to the Nave. We sat in the quiet and contemplated, expectantly. From the silence the divine strains of Allegri's "Miserere" began to fill the air, the notes rising to the vaulted Nave ceiling, flowing over the ancient stone screen and fluttering down on us like angel's wings. The music seeped into our souls, creating a deep sense of peace, as if we had been touched by God himself.

The worship over, we explored. The Ambulatories round the Quire were labyrinthine. Little chapels led off. One celebrated the musicians of the cathedral in stained glass windows. The large Lady Chapel was enclosed in delicate, incredible walls of glass.

An inconspicuous door led from the Nave into the cloisters with their stunning vaulted ceilings, stained glass, lavatorium and peaceful garden.

We walked across the garden, stood in the stillness gazing up at the superbly proportioned Tower and wondered why we had waited so long to visit such an awe-inspiring place.

South Quire Aisle - Window
"The outpouring of the Holy Spirit"

Bristol Cathedral

27 February 2007   *with Dave*

We caught the bus from Chipping Sodbury, where Dave's sister lived, into Bristol. There was to be an organ recital at the cathedral, given by Gerard Lee, Award Winner at the Oundle for Organists Summer School, 2005. He was now an organ scholar at Lady Margaret Hall, Oxford, and reading classics: young and very talented.

Programme:
Concerto in A minor (1st. Movement). *J S Bach*
Voluntary. *Thomas Tomkins*
Prelude, Fugue and Variations. *Cesar Franck*
Prelude No.3 in G major (Sat, Op 105). *C V Stanford*
Fantasia & Fugue in C minor (BWV) 537). *J S Bach*
Psalm & Prelude No. 1 (set 1). *Herbert Howells*
Toccata Primi Toni. *Einar Traerup Sark*

The last item was very exciting and interesting.

The most striking feature of the cathedral was that the Nave and Aisles were the same height as the Quire and its Aisles. This, uniquely, made the ceiling a similar height along the whole length of the cathedral. It gave it a sense of vastness and space. According to the Guidebook, this was known as a 'hall church'.

In the Quire were lovely misericords – a number displaying carvings of my favourite theme – the Fox and Geese, which appeared in various guises. For example one had the Fox (representing a clergyman) in the pulpit preaching to the Geese (lay people). Tapestry cushions on the seats above the misericords depicted the same design as the carving beneath, precluding the necessity to lift the fragile seats unduly.

There were various depictions of the Madonna and child. One of the loveliest, which included Joseph, was tucked away in a small alcove.

The stained glass windows had interesting themes. At the east end of the South Quire Aisle, we were particularly attracted to a window by Keith New, portraying the outpouring of the Holy Spirit on the disciples at Pentecost. It was a modern (1962), angular work with striking use of red stained glass. The South Quire Aisle itself had very beautiful vaulting and some intriguing faces carved on the supporting arches.

On our way out, Dave drew my attention to a series of windows in the north wall of the Nave. They were instructive memorials to the Home Front workers in the 2nd World War such as nurses, firemen, ambulance men and the Home Guard.

The Eastern tour

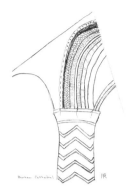

Durham Cathedral

9th June 2007 *with Dave*

Muted sound wafted across the Palace Green, the air was peppered with Geordie accents. The mighty walls and towers spoke of a fortress church, a safe stronghold. Inside, the lofty Nave was supported by massive pillars which led towards the delicate screen hardly dividing Nave from Quire. The West Rose Window glowed like oxygenated fire.

A modest door in the South Transept led to the Central Tower. We climbed the 325 narrow steps, pressing ourselves against the wall to let those coming down pass by. Relieved to reach the top we shared the panoramic view across the city - to the castle, the river and beyond - with about half a dozen other intrepid visitors. Then down the endless spiral case once more, to find ourselves gratefully on solid ground.

I now sought out my passion - the misericords. For some reason the guides were a little reluctant to show them to me. Only one was medieval (the other pre-Cromwell seats having been consumed by fire in the Civil War) – the remaining thirty seven were 17th century, somehow more formulaic and lacking the vitality of the medieval carving. In the Chapel of the Nine Altars, I found carving of a different sort - Fenwick Lawson's controversial sculpture made from massive trunks of beech, moulded into the image of Christ with carved hands and feet and the suggestion of a face, his mother by His side, reaching to his outstretched hand - Death and Resurrection. I loved the minimalism displayed.

Sunlight poured through the stained glass windows, bathing the floor in coloured light. Durham Cathedral was quietly noisy, with many visitors,

from children to grandmothers. A vast display of paper flowers, representing each diocesan church, stood near the North Door reminders of the cathedral's wider links. And then the organ started playing, rehearsing for a celebration later on: for this was 'Friends of the Cathedral' day.

The carved hand   Quire, Ripon Cathedral.

Ripon Cathedral

10th June 2007   *with Dave*

We stayed Saturday night at the Retreat and Conference Centre, Scargill, Upper Wharfedale, where one of our old university friends was centre manager. It held fond memories for us.

The next morning we made our way the thirty or so miles to Ripon. The memorable drive, through fields of poppies and across the beautiful bleak dales and moors, was a good preparation for worship at Ripon Cathedral. Red and gold banners bedecked the pillars in the Nave, where the service was to be held. The friendly congregation welcomed us to the Parish Eucharist, presided over by the Dean. A husband and wife read the Lessons – from 1 Kings (the widow of Zarephath) and Galatians (Paul's description of his conversion), along with the Gospel reading about the raising of the widow's son at Nain. Basing his sermon on these readings, Canon Michael, the preacher, chose the concept of 'Going out into the deep' as his theme; stating that the readings illustrated the contrast between faith and security, and that the character of faith was risk-taking. God constantly responded when people took risks in faith.

After the service, we enjoyed talking to some of the regulars over coffee and delicious homemade ginger biscuits.

As it was Sunday, the cathedral shop was not open so we were unable to buy a new Guide Book. Instead I used the Pitkin Guide I'd bought when I visited with my parents in the 1960s.

The main features I noted especially this time were:

The thirty four exquisitely carved misericords

The expressive statues produced in sheet copper by York artist Harold Gosney

The carved hand, below the original organist's seat in the Quire, which was used for beating time (the only thing I remembered from my visit in the 1960s)

The thirty eight boxed cushions on the ledge seats around the perimeter of the Nave, telling the history of Ripon: a millennium project involving ninety embroiderers.

We decided to eat in Ripon, as we were not certain how busy our next destination, York, would be. It also gave us time to look round the outside of the cathedral before we continued on our journey. The contrast between the south wall of the Tower and the Nave (perpendicular c 1510) and the Tower's west wall and the south Transept (12th century) was of particular note.

Detail of deer heading to the
Chapter House

York Cathedral (Minster)

10th June 2007   *with Dave*

The Minster was bustling with people when we arrived from Ripon. A choir was rehearsing, followed by someone practising the organ. We were disconcerted by the pay desks in the Nave. However, we learnt that the Minster was planning a dedicated building outside for them.

As we didn't have a great deal of time, we opted to go round the Minster and up the Tower rather than visit the Undercroft, despite the recommendation of a number of friends. In contrast to Durham, there were fewer steps up the Tower. As we climbed, we had good views of the exterior of the Minster and across the tangled streets of York.

Back down in the Minster we headed for the Chapter House. Around the walls on the canopies above the seats were "a riot of funny faces, animals and mythical beasts" mostly carved from 1270 – 1280. The Chapter House roof was suspended from the exterior dome and was without the customary central column.

Apart from the Chapter House, our main focus was the stained glass windows. The Great East Window was larger than a tennis court and depicted scenes from the Bible in 117 panels. It was made between 1405 and 1408 by John Thornton of Coventry, who was paid £56 plus £10 for finishing on time! The Great West Window was light and delicate. The tracery formed a heart giving rise to the name "the Heart of Yorkshire". Originally built in 1338-9, the stonework required complete replacement in 1998. Likewise the Rose Window in the South Transept had to be

restored after the fire in 1984. Finally we viewed the Five Sisters Window in the North Transept which contained some of the oldest glass c1260, creating an intricate design in grey and green gusaille glass. Under the West Window were a string of statues called the Semaphore Saints but we couldn't quite work out what they were signalling, despite an explanatory leaflet.

I loved the beautiful tapestry In the North Quire Aisle depicting all the animals found in the Minster. One disappointment, however, was that there were no misericords, the Quire having been burnt extensively in 1829 when all the woodwork, roof and some of the stonework was lost.

The external stonework surrounding the West Door consisted of a series of nine inch statues known as the Genesis Order, created when the door was renovated in 1998. I was particularly intrigued by the sculpture of God's hands holding Adam and Eve.

The weather was beautiful, so after we had finished our visit to the Minster (and Minster shop) we sat for a short while in the delightful Dean's Park.

Overnight we stayed in Beverley and visited the Minster there: the 'finest non-cathedral in the country'.

Lincoln Cathedral from Vicar's Court.

Lincoln Cathedral

11th June 2007   *with Dave*

We left Beverley and took the Humber Bridge into Lincolnshire. It was one of those clear but hazy days, mist was rising from the river as we crossed and we could hardly see one end of the bridge from the other.

When we arrived at the cathedral we were ready for a cappuccino in the Cloister Café. We then took the path round the outside of the cathedral, past Tennyson's statue, to enter at the pay desk.

Children were everywhere. It was their Festival of Church Schools – noise and activity. There were workshops on organ pipes and bell-ringing, Mystery plays, the rites and rituals of the church, stained glass windows, bosses, carvings. The chairs were concentrated round the altar podium in the Nave, leaving a vast auditorium, where children skipped and jumped around and chatted excitedly. Christ would have approved.

Meanwhile we admired the Dean and Bishop's Eye Rose Windows gazing at each other in a blaze of colour across the North and South Transepts. The glowing colours of the far West Window made a wonderful setting for the High Altar with its stone arches.

In the ancient Quire, Misericords were hidden behind red ropes. No-one was available to reveal these fragile masterpieces. High in the arches above, the Lincoln Imp surveyed us cheekily.

Outside, elevated on a ledge on the south face of the Central Tower, a peregrine plucked a pigeon for its young.

As we were leaving, the children began settling on the Cloister green and in the park beyond, for a break and their picnic lunch. Although we could not see much of the cathedral that day, the visit was made memorable by the sheer joy of the children.

Central end of the West Front, Peterborough

Peterborough Cathedral

12th June 2007 *with Dave*

We began our visit at Becket's Coffee Shop, housed in the Becket Chapel. It was originally built to accommodate the relics of Thomas a Becket in order to attract pilgrims. The money raised helped pay for the completion of the abbey at the end of the 12th century. We enjoyed cappuccinos on the terrace while we studied the Guidebook.

The glorious West Front was draped in netting. Inside there was less stained glass, and the cathedral appeared more ancient and less ornate, than many we had seen so far. The Nave seemed massive as there was no Quire screen. This had been removed and now surrounded the Treasury. A huge rood figure was suspended at the end of the Nave and painted lozenges, depicting the Fall and Redemption, Church and State, and Medieval Music and Arts, decorated the painted wooden ceiling.

There were no misericords. These had been burnt by Parliamentarian soldiers in 1643 at the start of the Civil War. Many years later the Victorians replaced them with their own carved seats and screens.

Two queens had been buried in Peterborough Cathedral – Katherine of Aragon (in 1536), first wife of Henry VIII, who had one daughter, Mary Tudor, who died at Kimbolton Castle. The other was Mary, Queen of Scots (in 1587) who was executed in Fotheringay Castle: her remains were later moved to Westminster Abbey on the orders of her son, James I. At the end of the 15th century and beginning of 16th century an Ambulatory was added by Abbot Robert Kirkton, who decorated its frieze with his rebus (a pun in stone, featuring a kirk and tun and the initials A and R). This Ambulatory was known as the 'new buildings'. It had exquisite vaulting - an almost identical design was later used by the architect John Wastell for Kings College, Cambridge.

We found Peterborough Cathedral an agreeably quiet and solemn place. On this day, even the girl singers, coming to rehearse, were muted in their dress and song.

ELY CATHEDRAL - The Ship of the Fens

Ely Cathedral

13th June 2007

with Dave

This time we had a guide – a cathedral lady who shared her knowledge lovingly and with great skill. Five minutes into her tour, a loud bell rang and we were called to the hourly prayer. She sat us down by the priest. Above us towered the Lantern Tower held within the Octagon, a superb masterpiece of engineering, "Moment of supreme creative vision", disaster turned to beauty. The Norman Tower having collapsed in 1322, the Octagon and Lantern Tower were brilliantly conceived by Alan de Walshingham and William Hurley, master carpenter.

The wooden ceiling of the Nave was a Victorian design, painted by two highly gifted amateurs, Le Strange and Parry (Hubert Parry's father). Gilded angels in the decorative Transept ceilings kept watch above the glowing 18th century stained glass. The 14th century choir stalls were "jewels of the medieval carver's art". Sixty misericords depicted a wide variety of themes - biblical, mythological and secular.

About the time the Tower collapsed there was a demand for the Lady Chapel to be built, following the cult of the Virgin Mary. The Lady Chapel stood apart from the rest of the cathedral: a massive, light and open space, presided over by a very modern Virgin figure. Bright bosses extended across the vaulting above. Bridal veiling, from a Dance Performance the previous night, floated over half the floor, enhancing and filling this exquisite, light place.

Our guide told us some background history. Both Hereward the Wake and Oliver Cromwell were local to the cathedral and used it in their different ways. Cromwell's men created devastation in countless churches around the country, but he made them spare his local cathedral. St. Ethelreda was a founder of this 'Ship of the Fens'. Her wish was to live life as a nun. The Isle of Ely had been a dowry from her first marriage. Her father had made her marry again – Egfrid, a prince from Northumbria – against her will. St Ethelreda did not consummate the marriage and, in 673, fled to Ely, founding a dual monastery for monks and nuns.

After lunch I climbed the Lantern Tower. The angel panels lining it were gigantic. Hinged, they could be opened to a feast of colour below, showing light streaming through the stained glass windows in the Transepts. Outside, from the Tower, the cathedral clock and Alan de Walshingham's house, with its chimney like a Lantern Tower, were framed as cameos by the decorative stone parapet.

The Erpingham Gate

Norwich Cathedral

13th June 2007 *with Dave*

Arriving in Norwich at 4 pm, much later than we intended, we found a car park by the castle. It was quite a long walk to the cathedral and there was lots of traffic, various one way systems, and countless pedestrian crossings to negotiate. At last the Erpingham Gate came into sight and through it we spied the cathedral door, open wide, with the spacious, vaulted Nave displayed beyond. There was so much to see and we were pressed for time as Dave didn't want to be late at our B&B. No time for a cappuccino.

We viewed the cathedral looking at the features in groups: the Norman arches and clerestories lining the Nave; the intricate vaulting with its countless intriguing bosses; the beautifully carved misericords and panels in the Quire; the stained glass windows glorifying the vast Norman Apse. It was so frustrating that we couldn't linger to see more or look in more detail.

We hurried to the beautiful, peaceful, cool Cloisters with countless colourful bosses depicting fascinating tales from the Bible, incidents from the lives of saints, even imagery of the Green Man. There was such detail and humour. We remarked on the calm quietness although we were only a few hundred yards from the busy streets.

Cut into the Cloister's Green was a Labyrinth of stepping stones. A leaflet gave 10 reasons for walking the Labyrinth:

To give thanks

To solve a problem

To take time out

To dream

To seek guidance

To resolve a conflict

To grieve a loss

To release a fear

To pray and be with God

Or just for fun!

By cheating we reach its heart in a few minutes.

Before we left our eye was caught by a colourful exhibition, Paul Forsey's 'Step into the Picture': a fresh and naive interpretation of Illuminated Manuscripts. All in all, however, we didn't feel we'd done justice to this magnificent place.

St Edmundsbury Cathedral

16th June 2007   *with Dave*

We'd stopped at Bury St. Edmunds a number of times en route from Sutton Coldfield, our previous home, to Minsmere RSPB Reserve for bird watching trips. We had never realised that there was more than a ruined Abbey and its gardens. We certainly were unaware that the church in the background was a cathedral, so we almost missed visiting it on our Eastern Tour.

St. Edmundsbury Cathedral was St. James Parish Church until 1913. It seemed strikingly modern, although the Perpendicular Nave was built by John Wastell, five hundred years previously, in the same style as Kings College, Cambridge. In our travels we encountered quite a few examples of Wastell's work 'built in the style of Kings College, Cambridge'.

Later, in Victorian times, another famous architect, George Gilbert Scott, had a hand in other aspects of the cathedral, such as the hammer-beam styled roof of the Nave, and the font. The Quire was added in the twentieth century to make the church large enough to be a cathedral. They were still building into the 21st century. The Millennium Tower was completed, but the Cloisters and Chapel of the Transfiguration were still under construction.

We looked at all the features and then round an exhibition of local artists. We could find no cathedral café for our usual cappuccino, so we repaired to the prayerful presence of the gardens, which were filled with the scent of roses and lavender. There we found plaques about the history of the ruined abbey. Its greatest claim to fame was as the site where the barons met to compel King John to accept the Charter of Liberties, an unfulfilled proclamation of Henry I and a precursor of the Magna Carta.

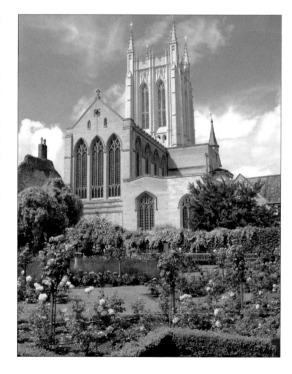

The August Trip

Wells Cathedral

2nd August 2007   *with Dave*

The rain was pelting down as we set off for Wells. We found a car park, not far from the cathedral, with an intriguing toilet which talked to you. It was accompanied by music from behind and warned you that your stay was time-limited.

At the door of the cathedral we waited to shake the rain from our coats. Inside we were greeted in a very friendly manner. We seemed to be the earliest visitors. My first impression was of the breathtaking view ahead. I was stunned by the scissor arches buttressing the columns: an amazing 14th century solution to the problem of the Crossing piers, which had started to sink under the weight of the tower. Gazing down the Nave I imagined the mystery of the Quire beyond, reached through a tiny arch.

We were in time for the famous clock to strike 9.45 am. At 10 o'clock a guide gathered three of us together for a tour. She was a precise woman, knowledgeable about every date and Bishop. She unfolded the secrets of the capitals decorating the pillars in the Nave. They depicted animals, plants and stories of local life. She explained that in winter, when work could not be done outside, the masons could come inside the cathedral, to carve decorations on specified areas around the columns to their own design.

Colourful canvas work decorated the Quire, embroidered by 120 workers from 1938 and all through the war. Disappointingly, we saw only four misericords – three displayed

on a wall, the other one as a seat – although the postcards in the shop indicated many more. Altar cloths hung round the Quire Transepts, brilliant designs for Christmas. The design for this season's Nave altar cloth was of Fish and Water.

The clock struck 11 am and this time we saw the higher figure, Jack Blandiver, ring the bell. There was one place we really wanted to see before we went - the beautiful vaulted Chapter House which was reached by climbing the ancient 'Heaven's Stairway'. It was amazing, with its central column blossoming "like an enormous flower or trumpet of praise."

The damaged Angel.   Exeter Cathedral

Exeter Cathedral

2nd August 2007

with Dave

Another guided tour. Our guide started by leading us outside to an area where the excavated foundations of an ancient chapel had stood uncovered until 1979. This was the church of St. Mary Major, once dedicated as a cathedral in 1050 and, like so many other buildings in the Cathedral Green, it was demolished in the 18th century to open out the view to the striking, ornate West Front.

Back inside the Nave, we admired the 'palm tree' columns and fan vaulting, sealed with colourful bosses, each heavier than a car. On the stone ledges either side of the Nave were the Exeter Roundels. Begun in 1983, stitched by 65 ladies, finished in 1989, they illustrated 2000 years of history both local and national. Moving to the Quire, we were told that, in the Second World War, stained glass windows and the Bishops Throne, considered one of the finest examples of Medieval wood carving, were moved piece by piece to save them from bombs. The Chapel of St. James fared less well. It was totally destroyed on 4 May 1942. On the wooden screen opposite, however, there was damage only to a small angel's head. Taking 18 years, St. James Chapel was finally re-built in the 1950s. Engagingly carved into the arches were the verger's one eyed cat, Tom and the rat he lost his eye over in a fight with an owl.

The guide amused us by showing us a door with a cat flap under the clock in the hollow North Transept Tower. Behind hung tassels attached to the bell ropes – a

magnet for mice. In the 15th century a cat was paid a penny a week to stop rats and mice infesting the Tower. He pointed out that the guidebook photo of the present cat, emerging from the cat flap, didn't show the sardines on the step in front of it, or the restraining hand behind the door holding its tail to achieve the purrfect shot. The cat was not amused and shot across the cathedral as soon as its tail was loosed. It took hours to find again.

The carvings in the Quire were 19th century by Brindley and Farmer, but below the seats around the edge were 13th century misericords. The most famous was behind the Bishop's Throne and was of an elephant, created from the carver's

imagination, with bovine feet and a rather interesting head.

Finally we moved to the South Transept where rows of wires hung from the ceiling. These were connected to the Bell Chamber. Thirteen bells could be chimed by one person without having to climb to the Bell Chamber.

WORCESTER CATHEDRAL - NORTH AISLE

The tomb of Sir John and Lady Jean Beauchamp of Powick.

The Black Swan appears on their coat of arms

Worcester Cathedral

7th August 2007   *with Dave and Vivian*

Accompanied by Vivian, an atheist but an enthusiastic culture vulture, we made our way to Worcester Cathedral. We decided to have a guide who turned out to be a deliberate man, full of knowledge, slow in delivery. We ambled round after him, mainly examining tombs. He gave us plenty of history and shocked us by saying that Cromwell's men used the Nave as stables in the Civil War. While he was talking, my eyes lighted on a magnificent stained glass window depicting scenes from the Dream of Gerontius, Sir Edward Elgar's most famous oratorio – a reminder of his connection with Worcester.

As well as the ancient tomb of King John with its weathered effigy, the guide pointed out two chantries in the chancel – one to Bishop William de Blois, who constructed the Lady Chapel in the 13th century, the other to Prince Arthur, who died in 1502 age.

A Victorian carved and highly decorated organ case had been positioned in the South Transept. It had been moved there to facilitate an uninterrupted view from the West End to the altar but, sadly, in so doing, obscured an interesting Jesse Window.

The guide led us down to the Undercroft, a calm and sacred space, which had been recently restored. Here there were new- found discoveries – a medieval pilgrim's staff and boots, and elements of the original 11th century cathedral.

Finally he took us to the Quire and the 14th century misericords, where he lifted a few for us to see the fascinating carvings.

By this time Vivian was in much need of lunch, so we repaired to the Prior's Pantry located in the cloisters. There we enjoyed soup, quiche and sandwiches, and a welcome cappuccino.

After lunch we climbed the Tower and admired the view over Worcester and around the shire to the Malvern, Clent and Lickey Hills. Immediately below we could see the waterlogged Worcestershire County Cricket ground, a victim of the recent floods which had rendered Tewksbury Abbey an island.

Crossing and Strainer   Carlisle Cathedral

Carlisle Cathedral

8th August 2007   *with Dave*

An almost full multi-storey car park was the nearest we could find to the cathedral. We had to drive to the top storey and from here we gained an interesting overview of the cathedral's structure.

Carlisle is an ancient cathedral with an ancient feel. We started our visit by studying the Guidebook in the Fratry Undercroft with a welcome cup of tea (rather than a cappuccino) in the Prior's Kitchen, which boasted Fairtrade, organic and locally sourced produce.

Refreshed we moved to the cathedral. The Nave was very short, the stones of half the original Nave were taken by Cromwell's men to repair the castle. It had austere pillars and distinctive rounded arches, some were distorted by the "subsidence of Roman deposits beneath a drying out of the foundations in a series of parched summers."

The Quire and Presbytery were the glory of the place. The striking 14th century barrel ceiling, decorated like the midnight sky with myriads of stars, had been re-designed and restored in 1856 and repainted in 1970. Around the Presbytery and the Quire were twelve columns, their capitals charmingly depicting the labours of a medieval farmer through the months of the year.

In the Quire every misericord was visible – a feast of carving. Faded early paintings, illustrating the lives of saints, decorated wooden panels in the North Aisle: but for intricacy and detail, the Brougham Triptych took the breath away.

Finally we returned to the Fratry where an art exhibition filled the hall. One imaginative work captured my attention. It featured Eilean Donan Castle, on the mainland near Skye, making me feel that it was time to return home.

The London Trip

St. Albans Cathedral

20th October 2007   *with Wendy, Ann and Mike*

At the age of seventeen, when I was a Ranger Guide, I made my first expedition to see the Abbey and Verulamium in St. Albans. Now I was returning over forty years later, while staying with Ann and Mike.

Led by Ann and her very basic leaflet, we entered through the renovated Chapter House. Immediately opposite, in the North Transept, we were greeted by the splendid Rose Window, funded by Laporte Industries of Luton.

We made our way past beautiful wall hangings, Water, Fire, Air and Earth, to the far end of the Nave. Noting the variety of styles of columns and arches, we were

aware of signs of extensions westward and of collapse on the south. I imagined medieval pilgrims, on their way to the shrine of St. Albans, gazing at the ancient murals on the Norman columns. Above the Nave altar, niches were filled with blue-clad statues of modern martyrs such as Romero, Bonhoeffer, Martin Luther King.

Back in the North Transept, Henry Moore's "Standing Figure" towered enigmatically to one side of the Chapel of Persecution. Another sculpture of two bandaged figures, depicted the "Price of Persecution". Out along the North Ambulatory, a massive brass of the cathedral's most famous abbot, De La Mare, dominated the floor.

Throughout our visit a group was rehearsing in the Quire, which stood bare of the organ and its pipes – away for renovation. We turned, therefore, to see the High Altar Screen, ornate with stone sculptures of Christ, the apostles, saints and clergy. To the side, the Ramryge Chantry had a poignant installation – six Angels of Grief – denial, anger, bargaining, depression, acceptance, peace.

The shrine of St. Alban with its Watching Tower was behind the High Altar. Here, the 13th century pilgrims would offer gifts in exchange for miraculous healing. Beyond that lay the Lady Chapel, restored by the Victorians, decorated with John Baker's beautiful carvings of plants and flowers. We found the delicate 12th century carving on the blind arcading in the South Transept also very attractive. Nearby, a replica of a small 1680 carved figure begging for alms directed us to the Poor Box.

The choir had ceased rehearsing and we went to examine the Quire stalls. Sadly there were no misericords.

Finally we took a look outside. The old Monastery Gateway and the imposing West Door provided a fitting backcloth to a wedding on this clear blue summer's day.

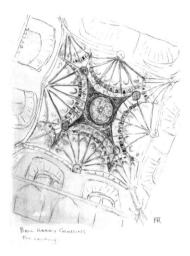

Bell Harry Crossing
For vaulting.

Canterbury Cathedral

22nd October 2007   *with Ann and Wendy*

After a two and a half hour journey from St. Albans we arrived in Canterbury ready for refreshments. Surprisingly there was no refectory at the cathedral, so we went to the 'Crypt' of Debenhams to peruse the Guidebook over a snack.

Returning to the cathedral, we were once more under Ann's excellent guidance. We began by viewing the lofty Nave, built over twenty eight years and completed under Prior Chillenden in 1407. A little way down stood the delicate Font reputedly smashed in 1643 by Puritans and painstakingly pieced together. The huge Pulpit featured saints associated with Canterbury.

Situated in the North West Transept, in the Martyrdom Chapel, the dramatic Altar of the Swords marked the exact spot where Thomas a Becket was murdered. From here we took steps down to the vast Crypt, dimly lit, with many side chapels. The ceiling of the Jesus Chapel had been restored. Early stained glass

portrayed the Crucifixion, and Madonna and Child. Other chapels had paintings, carved columns, beautiful icons. We ascended from the Crypt and found ourselves besides the Bell Harry Tower. Strainer arches had been required to take the weight of the columns. High above, the Crossing was decorated with exquisite fan-vaulting, like layered petticoats.

Stained glass windows abounded – dazzling medieval colours, particularly striking blues – the Poor Man's Bible. Most striking were the 13th century Miracle Windows in the Trinity Chapel, showing episodes from the life of Thomas a Becket. They seemed like tapestries in glass. Stunning stained glass windows adorned the South East Transept - the modern day work of Ervin Bossany, a Hungarian refugee.

St Augustine's chair stood in the Corona Chapel at the East End. Every Archbishop of Canterbury had been enthroned there. The Black Prince's tomb was also housed there, including an effigy of his dog, a strange, pig-like creature. Moving to the Quire I was pleased to note that there were a few misericords.

Our tour inside ended in the South West Transept, admiring the Great South Window with its complex figures from the ancestry of Jesus.

Our last act was to take a look round the exterior at the Candle Tower with its gargoyles. A kind man directed us further, to the Cloisters and Chapter House, as we negotiated this vast building. In the Cloisters there was a moving exhibition called "Fragments" – sculptures of damaged torsos – to raise funds for 'No More Landmines'.

The Font (designed by George Fredrick Bodley 1900)
and smith canopy (designed by Walter Hare)

Southwark Cathedral

23rd October 2007   *with Ann, Wendy and Claire*

Following an exhilarating 'flight' on the London Eye, we walked along the South
Bank, excited by its restaurants, theatres, bridges and human statues. Hidden
amongst office buildings we found Southwark Cathedral, old and new.

The cathedral seemed to be more about
people than architecture. As we entered,
just inside the South West Door, there
was a memorial to those who lost their
lives on the Marchioness in 1989 – fifty
one people, mainly in their twenties,
celebrating on the Thames.

Throughout our visit we were accompanied
by the lovely music of a violinist and
pianist rehearsing for a concert .We began
at the Font, crowned by a carved, golden
canopy. Behind it stood 15th century
bosses, striking in their primitive vigour –
Judas swallowed by the Devil, the Pelican
in her piety.

In the South Aisle of the Nave there was a memorial to William Shakespeare, depicting him at rest in Bankside Meadow, above him, a riotous stained glass window of characters from his plays. Throughout the church there were countless monuments to benefactors. Probably the quirkiest was that of the amusing Lionel Lockyer, a quack doctor with a poetic turn.

The oldest part, the Retro-Choir, housed four small chapels including the Lady Chapel. It had had a chequered history. In Elizabeth I's time it was screened off and let to a baker, until it was discovered that he was also keeping pigs in the building.

The Crossing was painted in muted colours and incorporated bosses from the 15th century. Below it hung a striking 17th century chandelier.

One chapel was particularly interesting. It was dedicated to John Harvard (1607-1638), the founder of Harvard University.

More people, famous inhabitants of Southwark, were commemorated in the windows along the North Aisle – Chaucer, Bunyan, Samuel Johnson. On the wall there was also a colourful map of Zimbabwe in acrylics and mixed media, including beadwork, created by Mbuyisa Mphalala: a reminder of the difficult situation there in 2007.

The North West Door led into the new building, where we found a well appointed refectory and welcome cappuccino and cakes.

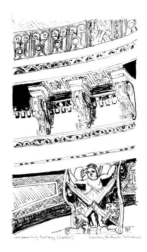

London, St. Paul's Cathedral

24th October 2007   *with Claire*

After viewing 'The Crack' at Tate Modern we crossed the Millennium Bridge to St. Pauls. Thanks to a Network Rail 'two for the price of one' offer, we both got into the cathedral for £9.50.

Claire looked round the ground floor, while I climbed to the galleries above to get a better picture. In the Whispering Gallery (up 259 steps) a disembodied voice said, "No cameras, please. No photos in St. Pauls." I felt a little cheated as I hadn't had this response in any of the other cathedrals.

Outside, after 378 steps, I reached the Stone gallery with views across London. These could be photographed.

Up a further 202 steps (580 steps in all) on narrow stone stairs and a metal spiral staircase between inner and outer Domes, I emerged on to the crowded Golden Gallery. Here the views surpassed those from the London Eye.

When I returned to ground level, I found Claire on a guided tour. I joined her just as they had reached the magnificent, incredibly elaborate Dome. The tour finished at the wonderful paintings by Sergei Chepik. He himself appeared in one.

The whole place dripped with war monuments and ornate ceilings in sparkling mosaics. Claire's reaction was like mine – a dislike of the strident, military feel – too many statues to generals and war, too few references to the simple Gospel. Our problem was perhaps summed up in Wren's epitaph:

"Beneath lies buried the founder of this church and city, Christopher Wren, who lived more than 90 years, not for himself but for the public good. Reader, if you seek his monument, look around you."

St. Paul's seemed essentially to be a monument to Wren. But what of the founder of the Christian faith?

We followed the signs downstairs to the shop and cafe, through the crypt, where there were more monuments and tombs, including the massive tomb of Nelson. The cafe was too expensive for us, so we headed back up to the cathedral level. On the way out, somehow too late, we noticed Holbein Hunt's iconic painting, "The Light of the World".

At the exit a sign, which we found sadly ironic, said, *"Hope you leave inspired and refreshed"*.

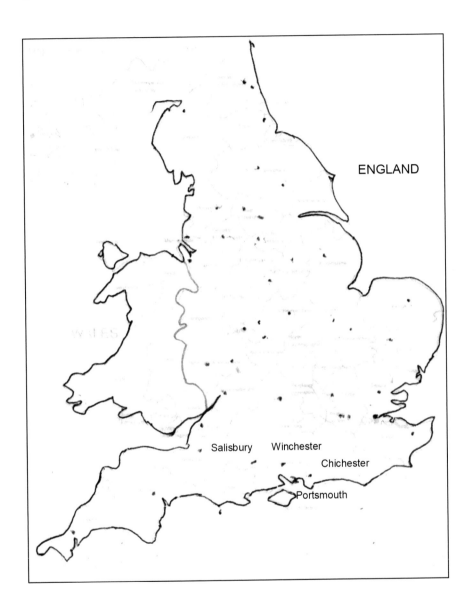

The Southern Tour

Salisbury Cathedral

1st April 2008

with Dave

As we didn't know Salisbury we decided to 'Park and Ride'. The bus took us to the centre but, alarmingly, sailed past the cathedral. We worked our way back and found the 'cathedral set in meadows'. We immediately located the refectory

in the Cloisters and adjourned to study the Guidebook over our customary cappuccinos. From our table we glimpsed the Spire, through the specially designed glass roof, beckoning us to explore the cathedral.

The most striking feature, on entering the Nave, was the vivid blue 'Prisoners of Conscience' East Window. There was no Quire screen, so the stunning glass could be seen down the full length of the Nave. In the north Aisle there was a fascinating model showing the various Lodges of craftsmen building the cathedral. It reminded me of one of my favourite books, Edith Pargeter's "The Heaven Tree", the tragic story unfolding as the mason grapples to build a masterpiece for his patron but is dogged by passion and jealousy.

The place was full of French school children chaperoned by eager guides and teachers instructing them on every detail. It made it difficult for us to see the cathedral in an orderly way. I arrived at the poignant 'Prisoners of Conscience' Window just as a guide was pointing out a crowing cock hidden among the faces. Amongst the gaggle of students, sadly, some of the children look bored. Beneath the window the frontals for the High Altar were dazzling, particularly the 'Energy' design.

As usual I went to the Quire to seek out the misericords, but was able to view only two very simple ones, the others being too frail.

The Spire's weight had taken its toll, requiring elegant bracing arches. These also provided the only example of the Perpendicular style in the otherwise Early Gothic architecture of the cathedral.

We reached the Chapter House through the peaceful Cloisters and encountered two wonderful features. Firstly, around the wall was a vivid frieze depicting scenes from Genesis and Exodus in exquisite carved detail. Carved heads also adorned the arches of the arcade, including one with three faces. The other feature was an opportunity to see one of the four original copies of the Magna Carta.

Since we were not sure where the bus stop was, we wisely decided to walk back to the 'Park and Ride' car park. We didn't see any buses along the way.

Winchester Nave with its Spine-like Vault

Winchester Cathedral

1st April 2008   *with Dave*

At lunchtime we drove between Salisbury and Winchester. Appropriately there was a programme on the car radio about the history of church choirs, with fascinating details about monastic and church life. This time we found a car park in the city and walked to the cathedral through the shops. Inevitably we began with refreshments in the Visitors' Centre, while we studied the Guidebook before entering the cathedral.

Glorious banners hung in the Nave, still in place after marking the 450th Anniversary of the marriage of Mary Tudor to Philip of Spain in 1554. The Nave was long and light. The vaulting had been described as "the spine of this great church." The Side Aisle Windows interested me – they had been transformed from Norman Arches into large Perpendicular Traceries, flooding the space below with light through both stained glass and gleaming plain panes.

I was thrilled to discover that Jane Austen was buried here. It was an unassuming grave in the North Nave Aisle, suggesting she had been a modest and devout woman. Incredibly, mention of her writings only came as an afterthought with a window above and a plaque nearby. In her time she would have known the 12th century font close by, carved with scenes from the life of St. Nicholas.

The Quire was a banquet of carving: animals and figures carved into the stalls and finely carved misericords, four of which were visible. I also loved the delicate Victorian Quire Screen, ornate with flowers and leaves, designed by the ubiquitous cathedral architect, George Gilbert Scott.

Above the Presbytery walls, six chests containing the bones of early kings, bishops and a queen, gave this building a special sense of history. As did the amazing 12th century wall painting in the Holy Sepulchre Chapel. As with St. Albans, it was remarkable to think that medieval pilgrims, on their way to the Shrine of St. Swithun, would have seen this.

The crypt was closed through flooding, but I managed to glimpse Antony Gormley's "Sound II" through the bars. The cathedral owed much to a diver, William Walker, who spent from 1906–11 on the dangerous task of underpinning the cathedral's waterlogged foundations.

Sadly there was not time to see the famous 12th century Winchester Bible.

The "Tree of Life" door designed
by Professor Bryan Kneale

Portsmouth Cathedral

2nd April 2008   *with Dave*

Threading our way through the streets of Portsmouth, we eventually spotted signs for the cathedral which followed the route to the historic part of the city. We were able to park at the Hovercraft Terminal and, on our way to the cathedral, walked close to the promenade where Nelson had paced the night before setting sail for Trafalgar. The cathedral was situated in a quiet street. It seemed a gentle, peaceful building, somehow timeless, combining old with new in a serene and calm beauty.

The interior was light. The arches gave a sense of openness and continuity. In the Nave the most striking feature was the sunken area, which lent it a Roman feel. In fact it was only completed in 1991. The West Door, the formal entrance to the cathedral, had an attractive modern 'Tree of Life' design complementing the simple Rose Window above.

The cathedral had an interesting overall design. The Baptistry was under the Organ Gallery and the Tower. In the North Nave Aisle, however, there was another font, placed under a stained glass window. The resulting kaleidoscope of light was reflected pleasingly in water placed in the bowl below.

One of the Daily Services was taking place in the Chapel of St. Thomas, so our visit was restricted in that part of the cathedral. In 1180, Jean de Grisors gave the land to build a chapel to honour St. Thomas a Becket of Canterbury, who had been martyred ten years previously. The chapel became a Parish Church in the 14th century and a cathedral in the 20th century.

To the north of the chapel of St. Thomas was the Lady Chapel, where there was an icon of Our Lady of the Sign (Isaiah 7 v14) by the famous Sergei Fyodorov (he had also created an iconostasis for Winchester and icons for St. Pauls). To the south of the Chapel of St. Thomas was the Chapel of Healing and Reconciliation, which I found particularly beautiful especially since it was, significantly, arranged in the round.

We returned to the car. Looking back we could see the cathedral with the ruined Garrison Church in the foreground and the 20th century Spinnaker Tower in the distance. Old and new seemed to be held together by the cathedral, whose own story, like all cathedrals, celebrated both its history and its continuity.

Chichester Cathedral

3rd April 2008   *with Dave*

It was the rush hour when we made our way to find the car park and the cathedral. Following a hunch, Dave took us on a round tour to avoid the traffic jams. Amazingly, we ended up at the Avenue de Chartres in a 'designer' car park. From there we could see the cathedral Spire through the besom-like branches of the bare trees. We walked through the shopping centre to West Street, where a free standing Bell Tower stood next to the Cathedral.

Again, we experienced that sense of peace as we entered through the Cloisters. Looking up at the Tower, I commented to Dave that he was unlikely to see a peregrine as he had in Lincoln. A man approaching us overheard me. "Oh yes you will. It's up on the pinnacle by the Spire and the nest is in the little turret." Dave suddenly found Chichester Cathedral very interesting.

We were greeted at the door by a guide. He commented that visitors had found the cathedral warm. Gazing down the length of the Nave and through the clean-cut Arundel Quire Screen to the dazzlingly warm colours of the Benker-Schirmer Tapestry, I saw what he meant.

The cathedral embodied the ancient and the modern: the centuries old architecture was harmonious and elegant, while the contemporary paintings, sculptures and tapestries were intense, deep and passionate. At the Baptistry, a font sculpted in Cornish stone by John Skelton, was complemented by Hans Feibusch's painting "The Baptism of Christ": while positioned at the opposite end of the South Nave Aisle was Graham Sutherland's poignant "Noli me tangere" (Touch me Not).

The 10.30 Communion Service was taking place so we could not get a close look at the Benker-Schirmer Tapestry However, we were able to admire the Chagall Window, depicting Psalm 150 in brilliant reds, yellows, blues and greens. We by-passed the Quire. None of the misericords were visible.

The Lady Chapel was closed off for renovation by a screen depicting its interior. Nearby was a moving sculpture, "Refugee", by Diane Brandenberg. On our way out, we took a look at the statue of William Huskisson, one-time MP for Chichester, who was the first person to be killed in a railway accident in Britain. He was struck by Stephenson's Rocket at the opening of the Manchester and Liverpool Railway.

We repaired to the Cloisters cafe where there was a party of Italians chatting animatedly and enjoying their cappuccinos.

An Unexpected Visit

Epstein's bronze statue ST.MICHAEL and the DEVIL

Coventry Cathedral

6th April 2008   *with Dave*

An unexpected visit. On the last leg of our Southern Trip we had time to spare, when we discovered friends that we intended visiting, were away. Travelling along the M6 to our next destination, it occurred to us to take a detour to Coventry.

Memories flooded back as we approached the city. Now it seemed a bustling, faceless place of shops, traffic jams and litter. I could not help noticing the warning signs, "Do not tempt thieves by leaving property in your car"; "This ticket machine is alarmed and emptied every night"; "Do not leave your bag unattended." The last one was in the cathedral. I thought back to my West Midland Probation days in the 1980s and my colleagues battling with crime then on Coventry's difficult estates.

Arriving at the cathedral I recalled the time of excitement when it had been newly opened in 1962. The number of people wanting to visit it then was so vast that my father decided we would wait a year or two before we went. One of my Pitkin Guidebooks was from that visit. I remember the awe and controversy of Graham Sutherland's huge tapestry and how moving we found the beautiful Chapel of Gethsemane.

Today the place was filled with noise – drums and guitars blasting out – a preparation for the evening's event, a Praise Service for Hope 08.

We wandered around with only a leaflet, no Guidebook was available. It was Sunday and, ironically, there was no one to welcome us. I spoke to a member of the 'event', who filled me in enthusiastically about Hope 08. I wished him well, but felt I must be growing old. It seemed a far cry from the peaceful reverence and angelic music of Gloucester Cathedral. But Coventry was a very modern place by comparison.

Or was it? Beyond the glass West Screen incised with figures of Angels and Saints, and linked dramatically to the modern building, stood the ruins of the old cathedral, bombed and burned on 14 November 1940. The charred cross and Altar of Reconciliation spoke of resurrection and forgiveness. Around the walls were Hallowing Places: simple prayers marking the Guild Chapels, reminders of the everyday and also of medieval times. Somehow the Tower and Spire had remained intact to cast its shadow on the uncovered Nave, where modern sculptures – Jacob Epstein's "Ecce Homo" and Josefina de Vasconcello's "Reconciliation" – gave us pause for thought. This place might have been a ruin, but what history it held and what a presence of beauty and peace.

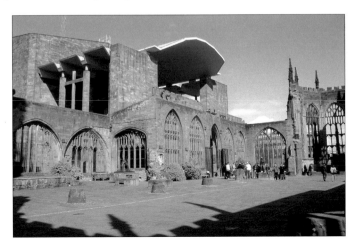

The Lenten Visits

1350s PATTERN REPAINTED IN THE (19th)

"The leopard of England and the fleur de lis of France were blended together to make a statement: England and France belong together under an English king."

Rochester Cathedral

16th March 2009   *with Ann*

We arrived by train, skirting the city, with previews of the cathedral and castle. There were reminders of Charles Dickens as we walked along the High Street. He died in Rochester and wanted to be buried there rather than Westminster. Turning left into the cathedral grounds, we immediately saw the signpost for the College Coffee Shop, where we enjoyed a cappuccino and bakewell slice.

We entered by the West Door and were met with haze and incense. The sunlight pierced the haze, seeming to underline the fact that this was the second oldest cathedral in the country. It was Lent and, throughout the church, the crucifixes and altars had been covered to mark the season. The Norman, Romanesque Nave with its rounded arches was simple and dignified. Ann pointed out some of the features – the ornate Quire Screen with elaborately painted organ pipes and eight statues in niches below; the ceiling of the Crossing above, decorated with Green Man bosses; icons either side of the Nave altar, one by the famous Sergei Fydorov; a fresh, bright modern fresco, combining depictions of both Jesus' and King Ethelbert's baptism -.also the work of Sergei Fydorov.

The Lady Chapel was in an interesting position, just off the Nave to the south. Large Perpendicular Windows gave it a light, spacious feeling. The altar cloth was modern with zigzags and arrows, described by one child as "converging on God".

Here also was a screen covered in a series of panels. Written on each were thought-provoking modern day versions of the Beatitudes, such as, "You're blessed when you're content with just who you are – no more – no less. That's the moment when you find yourself proud owners of everything that can't be bought."

On the north side, the Pilgrim Steps, worn down by 300 years of worshippers at William of Perth's Shrine, took us to the Quire. The surrounding walls were patterned with a design going back to the Hundred Years War, blending the leopard of England with the fleur de lys of France. Each leopard's tongue poked out to mock the fleur de lys. The Bishop's Throne was donated in 1877 by Lord Dudley, when Bishop Claughton moved to be the first Bishop of St. Albans, taking the Cathedra with him. There were no misericords. The Cromwellians had removed them. They also kept their horses in the Nave. A 13th century painting of half a Wheel of Fortune survived their attention, hidden behind the pulpit.

To complete our tour, we viewed the Crypt – a simple, peaceful place with a separate chapel dedicated to the Saxon Bishop, Ithamar.

The Tomb of Thomas Cantilupe

Hereford Cathedral

19th March 2009   *with Dave*

This visit was rather special. It was the first cathedral Dave promised to take me to, after he had recovered from his cancer operation. Leaving relatives in Bristol, we made our way in mist, over the Severn and down the Wye valley to Monmouth. Sunshine and blue skies reigned by the time we reached Tintern Abbey. We toured Monmouth trying to find the way out to Hereford, eventually leaving by a B road to Skenfrith, stopping at a pub for a cappuccino before the final leg to Hereford.

In Hereford we parked close to the cathedral, which was entered from the north by a two storeyed porch. Our first impression was of a stolid Nave with strong Norman pillars and rounded arches. They were hung with modern icon designs by a Scandinavian artist, Ludmila Pawlowska. The Triforium and Clerestory above were built 250 years later. The sunlit Font with its beautiful carvings was Norman. Sadly the carvings were defaced during the Reformation.

The North Transept housed the shrine to St. Thomas Cantilupe. Its colourful modern canopy contained an icon by Peter Murphy depicting "The Saint of Hereford in Heavenly Glory". Two textile hangings either side told of the saint's life. A beautiful Chantry in the North Quire Aisle, with elaborate vaulting and an interesting stained glass window, commemorated Bishop John Stanbury (1453 – 74). Disappointingly we were not able to access the Quire where there were over sixty misericords – 40 original and 20 Victorian.

Moving on to the Lady Chapel we were a little overwhelmed by the plethora of Ludmila Pawlowska's icons. They seemed to overfill the delicate space. There was more of Peter Murphy's vivid art work by the new shrine to King Ethelbert, to whom the cathedral was dedicated. Along one side of the Lady Chapel was an "artistic gem" from the Middle Ages known as the Audley Screen. Behind it was a tiny chapel, my favourite part of the cathedral, with four vivid stained glass windows celebrating the 17th century poet & cleric Thomas Traherne.

The stairs to the crypt led down to an oasis of calm and stillness. We finished our tour in the South Transept with John Piper's three lovely tapestries, showing trees from the Bible, set against the simple arched walls which had been built about 1107.

Before we left we treated ourselves to lunch of soup and coffee walnut cake at the Cloisters Cafe, in the daffodil-filled Chapter House garden.

Lichfield Cathedral

20th March 2009   *with Brenda*

We were slightly apprehensive as we took the train from Sutton Coldfield to Lichfield, following Brenda's £5 bargain, nightmare trip with the same company to London. However, we managed the seven mile journey without incident and walked in bright sunshine through the shopping precinct to the cathedral, with its wonderful Spires dominating the skyline. We began in the Coffee Shop opposite the cathedral for a pre-tour cappuccino.

Then we approached the cathedral from the west to admire the Front, with its countless statues. The sign at the door was friendly and stated that entry was free. A robed 'welcomer' handed us an informative Guide. We stood and looked down the Nave from the West Door. For the first time, I really took in the length of the building, through to the East Window in the Lady Chapel. The vaulting in the Nave was simple, but decorated with Bosses. The arches were pointed and lofty, with attractive Triforium and Clerestory above.

Not long after our arrival, children from the Cathedral School filed in for their annual singing competition. This year's pieces were, surprisingly, from "Mama Mia" – Dancing Queen, Waterloo. I scurried out of the Nave and into the North Transept, to view the Font. St. Stephen's tiny chapel led off this Transept. A distinctive curvilinear figure hung above the Altar. Passing the unique Pedilavium, I then retreated into the Chapter House. This was an intimate space, with a single, central, vaulted pillar surrounded by stone seats along the walls, above which were carvings and one ancient mural. More carved heads could be seen in the North Quire Aisle, defaced by Cromwell's men.

From the Lady Chapel I looked back to the relics of St. Chad, behind the High Altar, and took in the view down the more complexly vaulted ceiling of the

Quire, to the plainer Nave ceiling. The High Altar - viewed from the Crossing through the delicate, Victorian Skidmore Screen - was covered in a plain cloth as a mark of Lent. Up a staircase above the Consistory Court off the South Quire Aisle, was St. Chad's Chapel, where I sat listening, surreally, to the strains of Mama Mia and wondered what St. Chad would have made of it.

Back in the Nave, the children were finishing their competition. As I listened, I gazed at the lovely arches, curve after curve, carrying the sound to the East Window.

Five Unconnected Visits

The brass stag set in the paving of the crossing marks the original summit of Stag Hill, upon which the cathedral is built.

Guildford Cathedral

16th December 2009   *with Dave and Claire*

We first attempted to visit Guildford Cathedral as part of our Southern tour, but the University of Surrey was holding their Degree Ceremony. Now we were staying nearby with friends, on our way to visit our daughter and family in France. The weather had turned unexpectedly cold and it was beginning to snow when we arrived at the cathedral. We headed for the refectory, where we were served a good cappuccino – good froth, good coffee and an option regarding chocolate powder. Our table still had a white cloth laid from the previous evening's Friends Christmas Soiree. A group of people with learning disabilities, who seemed like regulars, came in. One came straight across to us and surprised us by asking, "Where's your car?"

The cathedral stood on Stag Hill, hence the stag emblem. It was consecrated in 1961. I felt I had a stake in it because we visited it when it was being built in the 1950s, and our family had paid for one of the bricks. Now we joked about which one it might be, noticing that those contributed by the Royal family had been highlighted. The interior was very simple, with a high Nave ceiling. Around the Nave were colourful friezes of the Nativity Story, produced by local Primary Schools. In the Quire a group of Secondary School girls were practising for their carol service, adding a lovely musical accompaniment to our tour.

There was a wonderful chart made by John Clark in 1954, when he was seventeen, with paintings of the cathedral and all the surrounding Parish Churches. Remarkably, also on display was an updated version he had created almost fifty years later, for the millennium. Nearby was a beautiful banner made by Miss I.L. Charleston in memory of her brother. It took her twenty five years to complete.

At the east end, the Lady Chapel was simple with a striking green ceiling. Above the Altar hung a life-size Madonna and Child in lignum vitae.

The unusual Children's Chapel in the South Quire Aisle was a poignant memorial to children of all ages 'loved, lost and commended to God'. Looking down the South Nave Aisle, the Baptistry could be seen with its spectacular canopy above the Font – three flights of seven gold doves, symbolising the seven gifts of the Spirit which came through baptism.

Just before we left, I took advantage of the toilets. A notice read, *"We are aware that there are shortcomings but at the moment we cannot afford the necessary alterations to the drainage. Contributions to the cost of plumbing would be welcome."*

Truro Cathedral

12th April 2010   *with Dave, Peter, Joy and Michael*

With my brother driving, we left Tavistock in bright sunshine and journeyed down the A390, stopping at Loswithiel for coffee. In Truro we found the nearest car park to the cathedral, it was virtually full and there was a bit of a battle to secure a place.

Michael was seated by the West Door reading the Guidebook when we arrived. Two interesting facts: Truro was the first new cathedral to be built in 600 years, the last being Salisbury in 1220; and in 1880, Bishop Benson devised the first Service of Nine Lessons and Carols.

We adjourned to the refectory for lunch and put the world to rights. My lunch was a delicious platter of Cornish cheeses, homemade pickle, salad and a granary roll followed by apple crumble tart and clotted cream.

Eventually we returned to the Victorian cathedral, starting at the west end to view the high vaulted Nave, leading the eye straight to the ornate High Altar. Down the South Aisle, stained glass windows included themes of the sea and commemorated John and Charles Wesley, of interest to me because of my Methodist upbringing. The Baptistry was dedicated to the missionary work of Henry Martyn (b1781). As it was Eastertide there was an Easter garden joyfully filling the small chapel next to the Baptistry. Beyond this was St. Mary's Aisle, which was skilfully incorporated from the original Parish Church by the architect J.L Pearson. It had a Barrel Roof with modern Bosses, a distinctive octagonal Pulpit, an ornate Triptych and a 17th century organ.

The Quire was decorated with elaborate carvings, as was the High Altar Reredos. Michael pointed out that the Quire was set at a slight angle to the Nave. In the North Quire Aisle we were fascinated by the extensive terracotta frieze, "The Way of the Cross", by George Tinworth. Dominating the North Aisle was another intriguing work called "Cornubia.– The Land of the Saints": a large painting by John Miller, of an aerial view of Cornwall and representing all the Parishes of the Diocese. From the Crossing we could see the three lovely Rose Windows, the West Window representing God the Father; the North Transept God the Son; and the South Transept God the Holy Spirit.

Outside, the Spire was in scaffolding. The limestone, of which it was made, was excellent for sculpting, but it was now eroding badly. There was a fear that it might not be possible to save this beautiful landmark.

Chelmsford Cathedral

17th December 2010   *with Ann and Mike*

We took the M25 from Ann and Mike's house in St. Albans. It was barely a month since Dave had died. We encountered a hold-up about a mile from the A12. While we waited we listened to Radio 3 to soothe us. Allegri's "Miserere" was being played. It took me back to Gloucester Cathedral and the ethereal experience Dave and I had had there. I shed a few tears. It seemed a providential way to spend the time trapped in this traffic jam. Eventually we arrived at Chelmsford, where the sun was shining and the sky was blue.

Until 1914 the cathedral had been a Parish Church (which dated back to the 13th Century). Our first view was of the highly ornate South Porch. Entering the cathedral, we were welcomed by Peter Ball's striking 'Christus Rex' figure. Beautiful high arches either side of the Nave helped to promote a sense of openness. I purchased a Guidebook at the shop next to the Chapel to St. Cedd's (to whom the cathedral was dedicated). Holy Communion was celebrated every week day in this calm space.

The Nave followed straight into the Chancel (there was no Quire screen), emphasising the space and airiness again. I was ambivalent about the modern black pulpit, which seemed strangely out of place in such a light, open space.

In the North Transept was a 'blind' window on which was painted a "Tree of Life" by Mark Cazalet – a huge Essex oak, dying on one side – a thought-provoking work of art, with fascinating details, challenging, amongst other things, our attitude to sustainability.

Next to a colourful 16th century monument to Thomas Mildmay was the Mildmay Chapel. The Altar Frontal in the chapel was an interesting Philip Sanderson Tapestry tracing St. Cedd's journey from Lindisfarne to nearby Bradwell where, in 654, he built a chapel, which can still be visited.

It was becoming more difficult to look round, as the choir from Chelmsford County High School had arrived for a last minute rehearsal for their Carol Service at 1.30 pm. I took a quick look at the patchwork "Glory" by Beryl Dean, beneath the East Window, and the Bishop's very modern Cathedra close by. The Chancel Organ was completed in 1995 and there was also an organ in the Nave, which was installed in 1994, the first completely new organ with mechanical action to be built in an Anglican cathedral.

We sat and listened to the delightful singing of the girls, before venturing out into the cold crisp day.

Derby Cathedral

1st April 2011   *with Les and Brenda*

We arrived in Derby early – about 9 am – parked the car and walked to the impressive Cathedral Quarter. Derby has spent a lot of money developing this area into a major shopping centre. It boasted award-winning food, a vibrant nightlife, beauty treatment, professional advice and "the city's rich tapestry of culture and heritage", stating that "buildings in the Cathedral Quarter date back to Tudor, Georgian and Victorian times and our crowning glory is the splendid Derby Cathedral with its 16th century 212ft tower." In fact the cathedral dates back to the 10th century, but as a Parish Church. It was elevated to Cathedral status in 1927, when there was a need for more Diocesan centres.

We started with coffee in the Cathedral Centre opposite. Downstairs, we discovered an interesting art exhibition depicting the Bible stories in modern day terms – the Flight into Egypt on a motor cycle, a hitchhiking Prodigal Son and so forth.

We crossed back to explore the cathedral, where there was already a number of school parties. Despite the age of the Tower, the interior was relatively recent, having been rebuilt in the early 18th century after previous considerable neglect. It reminded me of Birmingham Cathedral with its simple, classical style and light, open layout. The first thing that struck us was the Altar, with its Baldachin or Canopy, which could be viewed through the 'delicate-as-lace-and-intricate-as-a-fugue' wrought iron Bakewell Screen. This extended across the width of the lilac and white cathedral. On either side of the East Wall were the only two stained glass windows, designed by Ceri Richards to represent 'All Souls and All Saints'. The Retrochoir extension, built in 1972, fitted in admirably with the rest of the architecture.

Looking back to the West Door, we noted the gallery designed by James Gibb in 1733, which housed an impressive Compton Organ. On each side were further galleries, added in 1841. On the North Wall was a Consistory Court, in the past used to hear ecclesiastical legal questions, but now the home of the four-manual Organ Console.

Civic connections were emphasised by the Mayor and County Council pews, at the front of the Centre Aisle. They had elaborate, symbolic ironwork embellishments. One of the most interesting objects was the decorative Derby Plank, painted with moon, sun and starry skies, which was found in 1948 when repairs were being carried out. It possibly dated from the late 16th century. On leaving the cathedral, we had enough time to walk by the River Derwent to the Silk Mill Museum.

Oxford Cathedral

5th September 2011   *with Ann and Mike*

Staying again in St. Albans with Mike and Ann, we took the M25 and M40 to Oxford, coming off on the A41 to find the nearest 'Park and Ride'. On our 2nd attempt we found a place in the car park at Water Eaton. The bus into Oxford was diverted because of the annual St. Giles Fair. However we found the cathedral, Christ Church, St. Aldates, without trouble and bought cappuccino and croissant in the French run Croissant Shop opposite. There was no refectory at the cathedral.

The cathedral was an intrinsic part of Christ Church College and our tour took us round both. We entered the Cloisters through an arch in the Meadow Building paying £5.50p each for a concession ticket. Ann acted as our guide, beginning by pointing out the modern 'Tree of Life' and fountain in the Cloister garden. The building doubles as both the Cathedra for the Oxford Diocese and as the Chapel for the College – sometimes with a conflict of interest.

There is no Nave, as Cardinal Wolsey's men used the bricks for the college, which is based around the Green at the west end. The stained glass windows were the main

features. The stewards were eager for us to visit the stunningly vivid Burne-Jones window celebrating the life of the patron saint, St Frideswide. In the same part of the cathedral were some very old windows. One had glass of a green that could not be reproduced. Another had a depiction of Thomas a Becket, whose face had been blocked out by Henry VIII's men during the Reformation.

The Chancel and Quire were continuous: an intricate rib vaulting adorning the Chancel ceiling. We were intrigued by the Bell Altar which had a cross shape hewn out to leave a small arch at each side of the table. There were memorials to many famous people, like John Wesley and WH Auden. On the way out there was a fascinating window of Jonah and Ninevah – only Jonah was in stained glass, the rest had been painted on.

After a lunch of paninis and bagels in the Cafe Loco opposite, we returned to see the Great Hall, which was used daily as a dining area for the college. All round the walls were paintings of famous alumni – Gladstone, Pitt, Wolsey, Locke, Wesley.

We walked through Tom, Boar and Peckwater Quads, described as 'perfect architecture' (Tom Tower was designed by Christopher Wren) coming out in Boar Street. It was not far from the 'Park & Ride' bus. There was time to have a quick look round St. Giles Fair – rides, candy floss and lots of cuddly toys.

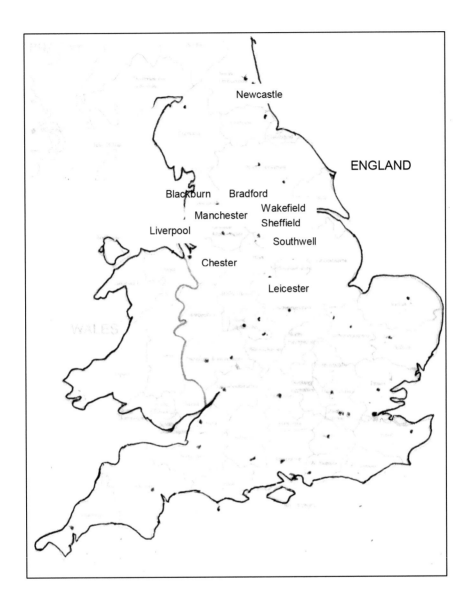

The Final Ten

Blackburn Cathedral

1st June 2012

After spending a week with the Bumnotes at the Swaledale Festival in Yorkshire, I made my way to Blackburn - the first of the 'industrial cathedrals'. The cathedral with its iconic fleche (slender spire), was easy to find from where I'd parked in Weir Street.

There was a lovely tranquil atmosphere on entering. The fresh openness of the Nave was achieved by the slender pillars and clear Swedish glass, as well as the simplicity of the vaulting. The floor was fascinating, consisting of slabs of fossil-inlayed Derbyshire limestone. I sat for some minutes, taking in the atmosphere and gazing at the' Crown of Thorns' over the Altar. Three figures could be seen through the archway beyond – a rood (Christ crucified), flanked by Mary his mother, and John. Around the walls were life-size paintings by Penny Warden entitled "The Journey", reflecting the Stations of the Cross. I found them striking but stylised. Behind me, over the West Door hung an immense figure of Christ the Worker by John Hayward. Below and nearby was the Mother's Union Banner, with Mary and the Baby set against the sky-line of Blackburn.

Eventually I moved on to the North Transept, and was stirred by a Josefina de Vasconcellos sculpture of Mary bathing her toddler son - from various angles her face expressed emotions of sadness, adoration, joy. The impressive organ was close by. Unusually it was open, displaying four manuals and six tiers of stops. In this Transept there was also the old Cathedra and eight lovely misericords.

I took a closer look at the beautiful Lantern Tower with its orange, yellow and blue Linda Walton stained glass panels, allowing light to stream onto the Altar. Suspended on pillars, high above and flanking the Altar, were contemporary six-winged Seraphim.

The Altar could be seen from north, south, east and west and had embroidered cloths on each side depicting symbolic birds – pelican, peacock, phoenix, and dove.

An Ambulatory ran between the Altar and the Jesus Chapel (not a Lady Chapel as the whole cathedral was dedicated to Mary). A vivid icon of 'Christ Emerging from the Tomb' dominated the chapel. The Altar cloth reflected the yellows and oranges in the painting. It was difficult to see much in this chapel because it is actively used for worship and prayer. Either side were glass panels with etchings reminiscent of Coventry Cathedral. In the Regimental Chapel, the Stained Glass Window used only the colours of military camouflage, as opposed to John Haworth's vibrant window in the South Transept.

Looking outside, I was not sure what to make of the massive fibre optic Globe symbolising the Healing of the Nations.

Icon representing the birth of the Christian Church when the coming of the Holy Spirit empowered the disciples after Christ's death

Bradford Cathedral

2nd June 2012

I was given a lift into Bradford and walked across the city to the cathedral, which was up a slight hill. It presided over a large hole, which should have been the new shopping complex. I approached the entrance through a stone arch and up a flight of stone stairs.

On entering, the atmosphere reminded me of a large Parish Church. Someone was arranging flowers, the choir was practising nearby, a group of girls were being taken to one of the chapels for confirmation classes and a lady was making up orange juice and putting out biscuits for the children. A church warden, emptying bins, found me a Guidebook.

For me the most interesting features of this cathedral were:

The four manual Organ, with nine tiers of stops

The Artspace with Rory Geoghegan's 'Spirituality in Sculpture' exhibition

The Chapel of the Holy Spirit, with its iconic painting 'The Coming of the Holy Spirit.'

The unexpected Plaque of the Anti Bolshevik Bloc of Nations to 'Freedom for Individuals'

The 2012 Candle

The Altar cloth in the Lady Chapel, with a beautifully embroidered figure of Christ the Shepherd surrounded by intertwining flowers

The Cross suspended on shark fishing line below a painted ceiling depicting sun and stars, and flanked by two statues, St. Peter and St. Paul, by local craftsman, Raymond Perkins.

I asked if I could obtain refreshments in the cathedral and was offered tea and coffee by the lady who had been making the orange juice. I joined a person sitting nearby poring over a pile of books. She was a 75 year old grandmother accompanying her granddaughter to the choir practice. Wakefield was really her diocese, but Bradford cathedral was nearer. She was also a Lay Reader and was preparing for her service the next day. Her theme was the Trinity, a difficult and confusing subject. This led us to a discussion of the theme of Trinity and the whole question of sermons – it was her dream to preach without notes one day. We had a lively and spirited conversation: a lovely way to end my visit to this warm, friendly cathedral.

The Lancashire Madonna, in her
millworker's shawl - MANCHESTER

Manchester Cathedral

2nd June 2012

I arrived in bustling Manchester at the end of a lovely train journey from Bradford, which passed through unexpectedly attractive Mill towns set in tree covered valleys.

The cathedral was very close to Victoria Station. On entering I was greeted by a young woman who obtained a Guidebook for me. After taking in the Nave, I looked at the stalls near the back. I was interested to know whether they had misericords and was referred to a small woman in her seventies. She took me to the Quire and enthusiastically showed me some of the best misericords I had seen so far.

She offered to guide me further. She was
a delightful, informative person and
I found her anecdotes and comments
more entertaining than the Guidebook.
She began by showing me the Frazer
Chapel, with its controversial picture
by Mark Cazelet of St. George and
St. Denys, in a triptych set against a
Manchester background. Then we
walked round the cathedral looking at
various features which she particularly
wanted me to see.

These included:

The Holy Night statue by Josefina
de Vasconcellos; a beautiful, delicate
resin sculpture, depicting an exhausted
Mary resting in the arm of Joseph, with
a contented baby Jesus nestling in his
other arm

The Fire Window in flaming red and
gold stained glass

The bejewelled contemporary Cross in
the Jesus Chapel

The beautiful swirling, dove-filled
Altar Cloth at the back of the altar

The four-sided swivel Lectern

The painting, 'The teaching of Christ', over the Chapter House Door, depicting the
Beatitudes in a modern setting.

The cathedral cafe was closed when I went to get my cappuccino at the end of my
visit, so I was directed to M&S's new cafe in the nearby temple to Mammon, a
busy shopping mall with the folks of Manchester rushing purposefully about their
business. There seemed to be a good relationship between the cathedral and the
people of Manchester – many locals came in to light candles or sit quietly while I
was there.

Wakefield Cathedral

3rd June 2012   *The Queen's Jubilee Weekend*

At about 2 pm I made my way down the motorway to Wakefield, in pouring rain. I had a little difficulty in locating a car park, ending up at the Trinity Walk Shopping centre, which was apt because it was Trinity Sunday.

I arrived at the cathedral just as they were winding down from the events of the morning – an optimistic Outdoor Service (which had had to be held in the cathedral) and a mass barbecue. Tea and coffee were being served in the hall adjacent to the cathedral. A friendly woman in front of me invited me to join her family at their table. She told me enthusiastically about the events of the day, despite the bad weather. She encouraged me to go into the cathedral to see a line dancing display in the Chancel. The Sanctuary was decorated with Union Jack balloons and the Altar was covered in Union Jacks, in the Jubilee spirit of the occasion.

I took a walk round the remaining area. Only part of the cathedral was open as, under Project 2013 (a scheme to make the cathedral more community friendly), the Nave was being totally refurbished with the help of lottery money.

The cathedral boasted 39 misericords in the Quire – 11 from about 1500; 22 from Victorian times, following restoration in 1860; and 6 added by the Edwardians in 1904. The Jubilee theme continued in St. Mark's Chapel, where there was a table

spread with a Union Jack
and memorabilia relating to
the Royal family. A bright,
almost primitive looking
mural, 'Three Saints' by Steve
Simpson, decorated one of the
walls. A further exhibition
of his work entitled 'Lenten
Images' stood nearby. More
artwork could be found in the
Chantry Chapel - an exhibition
of mosaics, inspired by the

cathedral's stained glass windows. A limestone sculpture of 'Madonna and Child',
carved by Ian Judd in 1986, welcomed visitors entering by the south door.

There was a temporary screen between the Quire and Nave, decorated with modern
iconic paintings. Looking through the viewing window, I could see a small digger
by one of the pillars, the floor had been removed and safety barriers surrounded
scaffolding and building materials. Near the viewing window, a model of the
Tower bore this verse:

"Our Spire is tall, our funds are low,
Please don't be shy, just have a go
Throw your change, whether pence or pound.
Aim at the bell & make it sound."

Outside, on the wall of
the Tower, a pictorial
ladder showed an angel
marking the fact that the
half way point had been
reached in their fund
raising. The cathedral had
also, optimistically, set up
a large screen. This was
for passers-by to watch
the Jubilee events. Sadly,
in the rain, everyone was
hurrying past and no-one
was watching it.

Bronze Anchor Memorial
(Stephen Broadbent)
THE CHAPEL of ST. GEORGE, SHEFFIELD

Sheffield Cathedral

4th June 2012   *Jubilee Bank Holiday Monday*

I found the city centre without difficulty and parked in Workhouse Lane. It was very quiet. Everything seemed closed for the Bank Holiday. I climbed the cobbled street up to the cathedral, having located it by the Spire.

I was taken aback by its cavernous vastness and loftiness. I didn't find it a beautiful building. Sadly there were no cathedral personnel anywhere either. I was welcomed by concrete and stone. A concrete extension, including a Lantern Tower, had been added to bring light to the dark Nave. Somehow it did not have the elegance of Blackburn or the majesty of Ely.

Parts of the cathedral, such as the Chancel, with its ceiling decorated with a choir of eight gilded angels, dated back to 1430. There had been much restoration in recent years. When the Parish Church became a cathedral, in 1914, it had been necessary to enlarge the building. This required the axis of the church to be turned 90 degrees which, in my view, had left the building lacking in harmony and unity. It felt unbalanced as I stood at the west end (with no West Door or window) looking down the Nave to the High Altar.

There were a selection of chapels around the Nave and Chancel. I found the Chapel of the Holy Spirit to be the most intriguing. It was intended to be the Lady Chapel in the re-orientated cathedral, but that was now next to the Sanctuary. It lay beyond and below the military Chapel of St. George with its bronze anchor memorial by Steven Broadbent. It had a beautiful, simple, vaulted roof with carved bosses of rose, vine, lily and sunflower motifs, witnessing the work of the Spirit in nature. However, I found the blue canopy below, designed by the architect, Nicholas Comper, somewhat incongruous. The entrance had more symbols alluding to the Holy Spirit – a Dove above the door and angels bearing the Spirit's message to the Seven Churches of Asia. The 'Te Deum' Window also reflected the theme, with flame-like tracery and a Dove at the apex, brooding over various aspects of creation below.

Throughout my visit I was conscious of the lovely scent of lilies pervading the cathedral. I was surprised to discover that it was the product of just two strategically placed elegant Jubilee flower arrangements. They added a welcome human touch to the otherwise impersonal experience.

SOUTHWELL MINSTER

Southwell Cathedral (Minster)

4th June 2012   *Jubilee Bank Holiday Monday*

Arriving in the tiny 'city' of Southwell in the afternoon, I made my way along the quaint streets to the Minster. A Jubilee Organ Recital was just starting. I was welcomed by a very friendly and helpful steward, inviting me to join the audience in the Nave. I would love to have accepted his invitation but, as I only had a short amount time, I decided to concentrate on viewing the Quire and east end.

The place felt ancient – it was built 900 years ago. I was impressed by the majestic Crossing. The Guidebook described its massive Norman Arches and Columns in terms of Philip Larkin's phrase – "a serious place on a serious earth." In the Tower above was the Ringing Chamber. The Guidebook pointed out that "the Southwell 'ring' is unusual, in that its twelve bells are rung in an anticlockwise direction."

In the Quire I was again unable to see any misericords, however, I was delighted to locate a small mouse on the Altar rail. It was the signature trademark of carver, Richard Thompson (Kilburn, South Yorks. 1949). I looked back to the Lectern and was able to see down the length of the wooden, barrel-like Nave roof. Nearby was the largest pulpit I had ever seen. Its 'spurs' were big enough to accommodate three preachers debating at the same time. I would like to have known more. There was, regrettably, only information about the pulpit in the Nave.

At the East End I explored the four chapels – the Airman's Chapel commemorating those who lost their lives in wars; the adjacent St. Thomas' Chapel, now used as a vestry by the clergy; the St. Oswald's Chapel, with an Altar Frontal designed by John Piper; and the Chapel of Christ the Light of the World, an ancient chantry now dedicated to prayer and reflection, where votive candles surrounded a poignant, primitive statue by Peter Ball. A most unusual contemporary depiction of fourteen Stations of the Cross, represented by small metal figures, stretched down the South Aisle of the Quire. It left me with food for thought, especially with its contrast in style to the other aspects of the Minster.

The Mother's Union Banner
LEICESTER CATHEDRAL

Leicester Cathedral

6th June 2012   *with Enid*

Enid and I took the train from Kettering. Enid had directions from the station to the cathedral, but they didn't seem to resemble any routes around us. So we followed our noses down Granby Street to the city centre. There we found an Information Office and were given instructions and maps. We didn't have to walk far before we were able to resort to 'following the Spire'.

As we entered through the churchyard we were enveloped in peace and calmness. At the cathedral door we were met by a spritely woman in a smart lightly striped, black suit. She was older than she looked. She engaged us in conversation and we learnt as much about her as we did about the cathedral. Originally from Ipswich, she had a delightful Suffolk accent. Her husband, however, came from Leicestershire and she now viewed the county as her home, moving to live there after he'd died. Eventually she issued me with a leaflet and I started to go round the cathedral. Enid continued to chat and asked to be shown any Green Man / Woman effigies. She was then also taken to see other features.

At the end of our visit I asked Enid for her impressions of the cathedral. She had been elated by the experience, having found the cathedral intimate, peaceful, safe and welcoming.

Here is her checklist of the most interesting features:

The Green Man/Woman Carving just behind the pulpit

The 3 carvings from the Guild Hall

The general medieval colour scheme, sympathetically restored by the Victorians

The wooden ceilings and gilded angels

The carvings of Grotesques ('people with ailments and discontents') high above the South Aisle

The massive Coronet made for the Queen's Jubilee visit in April 2012

The delicate Mothers' Union Banner

St. Katharine (Katharine Wheel)'s Chapel

The great East Memorial Window to those who died in the 1914-18 war

and The etching in the West Door of the Parting of the Red Sea with a leaping fish.

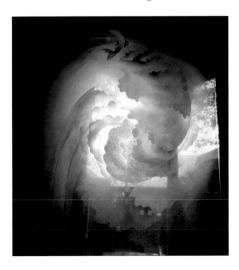

We both enjoyed the impromptu piano playing of 'As Time Goes By', 'The White Cliffs of Dover' and 'Jerusalem' by an elderly gentleman as we were about to leave.

We then found a nice teashop to have lunch and enthuse over our experience.

Carved 'Elephant'   Chester Cathedral

Chester Cathedral

20th June 2012   *with Rick*

We took the Upton 'Park and Ride' into the city centre. The bus stopped just round the corner from the famous Eastgate Clock.

The cathedral was nearby, entered through a labyrinth of corridors. The shop was closed for renovation, but we were able to buy a Guidebook from the ticket desk. We adjourned to the Refectory at once to study it over coffee. The Refectory was accessed from the Cloisters and was the same building in which the monks would have taken their meals in the 13th century. There was still the raised dais for the Abbot and important guests, and a striking Wall Pulpit from which inspiring readings would have been read during their silent meals. At the west end there was a stunning stained glass Creation Window designed by Rosalind Grimshaw.

Back at the entrance (£4.50 for over 60s) we were issued with earphones to listen to the high-tech radio commentary. I almost missed the Baptistry, with its Italian Font, which was behind a row of chairs. I stood under the West Window and looked down the vast Nave, the last part of which was begun in 1360 and not finished until 130 years later.

The great West Window behind me had vivid coloured glass and was a modern 1960s design by W.T. Carter Shapland. On the North Wall were interesting Pre-Raphaelite mosaic Murals of four Old Testament characters. There were neat Victorian mosaic floors in both the Lady Chapel and the Quire, and a beautiful intricate inlaid floor, designed by George Gilbert Scott, at the Crossing.

The Choir Stalls were delicately carved, including an 'elephant' from the Crusades, and there were excellent misericords.

Near the oldest part of the cathedral (a rounded Romanesque Arch in the North Transept), was a rare Tyrollian Cobweb Picture, painted on the 'net' of a caterpillar. By way of contrast, in the South Transept, the Children's Chapel was decorated with lively contemporary posters and life-size cut–outs of Noah and the animals.

The Chapter House led off the Cloisters and was part of the medieval Monastery. It was interesting that the monastery had been spared by Henry VIII. He needed Chester as a new Diocesan seat alongside the over-stretched Lichfield diocese.

The central garden of the Cloisters was very peaceful, with a delightful 20th century statue, 'The Water of Life', by Steven Broadhurst.

Chester was a cathedral with everything you could want – vibrant stained glass windows, superb carvings and so much more.

Carved Liver Bird. Choir stalls. LIVERPOOL

Liverpool Cathedral

21st June 2012 *with Rick*

It was not a good day to go to Liverpool. It was miserable, grey, drizzly weather and, apart from the area immediately round Lime Street Station, the city appeared miserable and grey. It took us about 20 minutes to walk to the huge Anglican Cathedral.

On entering I was totally confused. I felt as if I was in a shopping mall. The Central Space was being prepared for the local Radio Station's Regional Broadcasting Awards (RBA) and was filled with tables laid for the evening's event. Large screens, amps and wires surrounded the place. I was also overwhelmed by the sheer scale of

the cathedral. As was now my tradition, we made our way to the Cathedral Shop and Refectory, where we studied the Guidebook and drank cappuccinos.

Rick and I started our tour in the Quire, picking our way through the tables and cables, passing a Josefina de Vasconcellos fibre glass sculpture of the

Holy Family, similar to ones in Manchester and Blackburn. I was interested by the Liver Bird figures in various places – the floor of the Chancel, the steps of the Choir Stalls. The Cathedra, known here as the Bishop's Throne, was huge, as was the elaborate High Altar. The present Altar Frontal was a modern depiction of angels. There was a fondness for blue lighting, which illuminated the Bridge, the Organ Pipes and various other features.

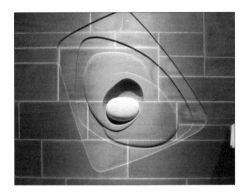

In the aisle at the side of the High Altar was a beautiful memorial to Bishop David Sheppard – white Portland stone set in the sandstone wall, "evoking a sense of intrigue and wonder" – designed by Steven Broadbent.

The Chapter House was a much simpler, less lofty place. It had an Altar, as if it were another chapel. There was an interesting view east down the length of the cathedral, through 'The Nostrils' in the Ambulatory. We were encouraged to go to the Lady Chapel, where the Greater Richmond Children's Choir from the USA was singing, as part of a tour of Britain and Ghana. The Lady Chapel seemed almost the size of some cathedrals. I listened for a few minutes and then left Rick, to finish my tour of the Cathedral. I tried to see the decorated ceiling of the Font in the Baptistry, but screens had been placed in front and caterers were preparing food. A steward explained to Rick that they took on these events to avoid having to charge people to go into the cathedral.

On our way out, we noticed Tracey Emin's 'Artwork,' "I felt you and I know you love me", just below the West Window. While looking at it, a magenta ghost car bizarrely appeared on a black dais by the door. Part of the RB Awards?

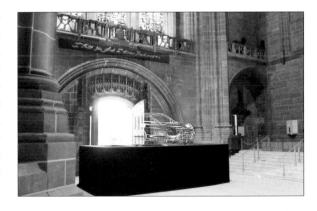

'First Supper' Medieval roundel depicting
Madonna feeding the Christ child
NEWCASTLE

Newcastle Cathedral

23rd June 2012

I was very excited, but ambivalent, about this, the last cathedral on my pilgrimage. I used my satnav, which directed me, in ever decreasing circles, to a car park in the city centre maze. I emerged, disorientated, on to a street... Pilgrim Street. I asked a passing couple the way to the cathedral. The man gave directions in terms of various Fast Food outlets. "Down that road, you'll see McDonalds on your right. Take the road with Pizzaland and KFC on either corner." On the way I spotted the cathedral's Crown Tower from time to time over, and through, shops and offices.

It was Saturday, so there were no cathedral personnel around, but there was a choir rehearsing, filling the cathedral with crystal notes and evocative Latin phrases. I bought a Guidebook and took a Welcome Leaflet, following the highlights it suggested. By the entrance door was a statue to the underrated Admiral Lord

Collingwood, who took control of the Battle of Trafalgar on Nelson's death, successfully concluding it. I took a photo of the early 15th century Font. Light defused between the Canopy and Font, giving it an ethereal air. Hanging from the Nave Pillars were six attractive banners depicting Fire, Water, Earth, The Tree of Life and The Crown Tower.

Before exploring the North Transept, I admired the elegant Uttoxeter-stone Pulpit. There was a Crypt (which was once a Charnel House storing bones and was now a storage room for furniture and traffic cones) leading off the North Transept. I loved the colourful, half hidden, modern Stained Glass Window at its entrance. St. George's Chapel was next to it. Here Stained Glass Windows celebrated two Tyneside Industrial Entrepreneurs, who both died in 1931. On the west wall, a vividly colourful 17th century monument commemorated William and Jane Hall and their six children.

Continuing round the cathedral, I really liked the simple translucent Danish Memorial Window, with crosses for Faith, Anchors for Hope and the heart for Charity, and the similar Chapel of Resurrection Window, with symbols of Christ's Passion – nails, chalice, scourge. The Incarnation Chapel had a wonderful bright Triptych of the Nativity. At the end of this area, above the Chapel of Ascension, was a third Window, in neat blues and reds.

Down the South Aisle, beautiful embroidered and lace cloths were displayed on wooden Chests. On the south wall was a Stained Glass Window depicting a renowned local chemist, Joseph Garnett, performing good works! In St. Margaret's Chapel I marvelled

at the tiny Virgin and Child roundel in the otherwise clear window: the only medieval stained glass to survive. I had been skirting the Quire but, now the rehearsal had finished, I was delighted to discover a plethora of misericords there, and the spectacular five tiered Canopy over the Bishop's Throne, skilfully carved by Ralph Hedley.

I was loath to leave this place which marked an end to my five year project. I decided to send myself a postcard with the message, "LEAVING HERE WILL TAKE ME ON A NEW PILGRIMAGE".

Reflections

The original idea was simple – visit all the Anglican cathedrals in England, in celebration of my sixtieth birthday. The actual experience was much more complex.

For a start, it led me to explore every corner of England – from the northern stronghold cathedrals of Carlisle and Durham, to the clotted cream outpost of Truro in the south-west and the ancient founding cathedral of Canterbury in the south east; and from Hereford near the western border, to the glorious eastern cathedrals of Ely and Norwich. Furthermore, it left me with wonderful memories of the journeys I'd made with Dave, particularly those down the east of the country and along the south coast.

It also helped me confront some of my prejudices and fears when, driving myself in every sense, I ventured into the 'industrial heart' of the country on the weekend of the Queen's Diamond Jubilee. Some surprises awaited me there: the beauty of Blackburn Cathedral, the lovely journey from Bradford to Manchester, the vision and enterprise of Wakefield Cathedral.

It transported me back in time. It took me to the disciplined life of the medieval monasteries: to prayer filled cloisters, where monks spent hours in deep contemplation and meditation; to ancient Quires, where the rigours of having to stand through daily worship were mitigated for the old and weak monks, by that merciful ledge, the misericord. I was reminded that the Church had been Roman Catholic then, and a central part of daily life. An illiterate majority learnt the Christian message through Bible stories in stained glass, and in the carvings around the cathedrals. The message then seemed harsh, with its emphasis on sin and the prospect of hell – a powerful way of controlling the masses. It was a time, too, when cathedrals had shrines where pilgrims would flock for healing and comfort, a substitute for modern medicine. An intriguing discovery, too, was that the money raised from their gifts was often used to build the beautiful Lady Chapels.

I learnt, too, that cathedrals were there at the start of the country's democracy. Back in the 13th century, the barons gathered at St. Edmunds Abbey, in Bury St. Edmunds, to hold King John to the Charter of Liberties, a precursor of the Magna Carta. Once the Magna Carta was signed, cathedrals were among the places where the first documents were housed. Original copies can still be seen in Durham, Hereford, Lincoln and Salisbury.

They were also radically affected by political change. Many cathedrals suffered in the English Reformation under Henry VIII's dissolution of the monasteries, and his tendency to asset strip their beautifully crafted furnishings. They fared no better during the English Civil War, when soldiers displayed a sacrilegious contempt by stabling their horses in the Naves of such cathedrals as Worcester, and taking the stones from cathedrals, such as Carlisle, to re-build castle defences. Saddest of all were the number of cathedrals which, either on religious grounds or out of sheer vandalism, were stripped of their carvings, stained glass windows, altars and screens during this period. Many of my beloved misericords disappeared at this time.

However, alongside all this destruction, I discovered inspiring examples of amazing creativity emerging from disaster. Ely's wonderful Lantern Tower and the beautiful Scissor Arches of Wells were both responses to collapsing towers and weak foundations. And in Coventry I was moved, as always, by the way in which the bombed ruins of the old cathedral had been retained, re-invented as a powerful symbol of reconciliation.

Above all, not unexpectedly, the experience also fed me spiritually. In up-holding the offices of the church and inviting visitors to share in hourly prayers throughout the day, cathedrals emphasise the link with religion. However, I was most moved by being surrounded by a cathedral's beauty and craftsmanship. I was particularly impressed by the thought that the work would have been done 'to the glory of God', and the idea that much of it was in places where it would never be seen.

On many occasions I had an unmistakeable sense of peace and calm as I entered a cathedral. I felt this particularly in the cloisters. It was as if the centuries of prayer had lingered in the atmosphere. Music also played its part, instrumental and sung. Overall, I would say that my most special and poignant memory was of the evensong in Gloucester Cathedral, when Dave and I felt touched by eternity. Remembering this has been a real comfort in my grieving process.

Although the cathedrals have had to reconcile being places of worship and appearing as a kind of art gallery/museum, they seemed in good heart. There had been significant changes since the 1950s, the most obvious being the entrance charge many now had to make. Somewhere, I read that it cost from about £3,000 to

£4,000 a day to maintain the life of a cathedral. Canterbury cost £9000. Some, like York and Wakefield, had ambitious new projects funded by the National Lottery. Many appeared to have thought actively about their relationship with present day society. They had opened their doors for all sorts of public events, from concerts to award ceremonies, and encouraged local schools and communities to feel at home in their awe-inspiring buildings. I encountered committed people of all ages for whom the cathedral was a family and a community. On the other hand, I also observed others who preferred to slip into its sanctuary anonymously: to sit quietly, light a candle, mull over a difficult decision.

My project to visit all the cathedrals is completed but it has led to a cornucopia of subjects to explore. I am particularly interested in the great variety of depictions of the Madonna; the place of shrines in medieval England; and how icons have become more prevalent in cathedrals. I would also like to seek out more about the artists and architects whose work I encountered. The list is endless.

I look forward to returning to many of the cathedrals – my initial visits often seemed rushed, although I probably took in only as much as I could cope with at the time. I look forward to sharing their beauty, richness and peace again with friends. And, of course, I look forward to enjoying a cappuccino in the cathedral 'Pantries' and 'Kitchens'. Perhaps I will see you there too.

Trish Rogers, 2013

Dates cathedrals established

AD

602	Canterbury		1836	Ripon
604	Rochester		1847	Manchester
604	London, St. Pauls		1877	St Albans
c627	York		1877	Truro
c642	Winchester		1882	Newcastle
c669	Lichfield		1884	Southwell
676	Hereford		1880	Liverpool
680	Worcester			*(Present building 1978)*
			1888	Wakefield
909	Wells			
			1905	Birmingham
			1905	Southwark
1050	Exeter		1914	St Edmundsbury
1072	Lincoln		1914	Chelmsford
1075	Salisbury		1914	Sheffield
	(Present site 1220)		1918	Coventry
1093	Durham			*(Present building 1962)*
1094	Norwich		1919	Bradford
			1926	Blackburn
1108	Chichester		1927	Derby
1109	Ely		1927	Leicester
1133	Carlisle		1927	Portsmouth
			1927	Guildford
				(Present building 1961)
1541	Peterborough			
1541	Gloucester			
1541	Chester			
1542	Bristol			
1546	Oxford			

Glossary

AMBULATORY (from the Latin *ambulare* 'to walk'). Procession way around the east end of a cathedral, behind the altar. Covered passageway around a cloister.

APSE (from the Latin *appsis* 'arch' or 'vault'). Semi-circular end to the chancel, often having a domed or vaulted roof.

BOSSES. Decorations, made of stone or wood, covering the rib intersections of vaulted ceilings.

CATHEDRA (from the Greek *kathedra* 'a seat'). A Bishop's seat or throne.

CHANCEL. The area around the High Altar at the east end of a cathedral.

CHANTRY. A Trust Fund to pay the clergy to say mass for the soul of a departed person to speed their soul to heaven.

CHANTRY CHAPEL. Chapel dedicated to the deceased, where the clergy would fulfil their chantry duties towards that person.

CLERESTORY. (Clear storey). Upper level of the Nave, rising above the rooflines of the lower aisles, and containing windows to bring in more light/air.

CONSISTORY COURT. A type of ecclesiastical court established by William the Conqueror, losing most of its power in mid 19th century. At one time it heard matrimonial and probate matters. Now it hears mainly churchyard and church property issues. Can deal with the misconduct of clergy.

CROSSING. Junction between Nave, Quire and the Transepts which form the cross shape of the cathedral, a tower, spire or dome often rises above it.

CRYPT (from the Latin *crypta* 'concealed, 'private'). An underground stone chamber, possibly containing coffins or relics.

DIOCESE (from the Greek meaning 'administration'). The district or see under the supervision of a Bishop, divided into Parishes covering the whole of England and Wales.

FRATRY (Carlisle Cathedral). A refectory. At Carlisle Cathedral, now houses the Friar's Kitchen Restaurant. Once part of the medieval priory, the main floor being the monks' dining hall.

LAVATORIUM. Monks communal wash area.

MISERICORD (mercy seat). A ledge, with medieval carvings, found on the underside of hinged seats situated in the Quire. Purpose to give some support to weaker monks' during long periods of standing during worship.

NAVE (from medieval Latin *navis* 'ship'). The main body of a cathedral, the name possibly comes from the keel shape of the vaulted ceiling.

PARISH (From the Old French *paroisse*). The basic unit of the Church of England and a sub-division of a Diocese. It represents both geographical location and a body of people.

PEDILAVIUM (Lichfield). An architectural feature constructed to be the site of the ritual feet washing associated with Maundy Thursday.

PRESBYTERY. Area reserved for clergy also known as 'chancel' or 'sanctuary'

QUIRE. The area, usually between the Chancel and the Nave, where the clergy and choir sit during services. Alternative spelling of 'Choir'.

RETROCHOIR. An area behind the High Altar, which often separates it from the end chapel/s.

SANCTUARY. The area around the High Altar, considered sacred because of its nearness to the physical presence of God in the form of the Eucharist (Holy Communion). May denote the entire worship area.

TRACERY. The stonework elements that support glass in Gothic windows.

TRANSEPT. An area set crosswise to the Nave, separating the nave from the Sanctuary.

TRIFORIUM. A shallow arched gallery, within the thickness of the inner wall, which stands above the Nave. It may occur at the level of the clerestory windows or below and may have an outer wall of glass rather than stone.

UNDERCROFT. Dating back to medieval times, it was traditionally used as a cellar or storage room. It is usually brick lined and vaulted.

VAULT. An arched stone ceiling.

Alphabetical list of cathedrals and websites

B

BIRMINGHAM www.birminghamcathedral.com
BLACKBURN www.blackburncathedral.com
BRADFORD www.bradfordcathedral.org
BRISTOL www.bristolcathedral.co.uk

C

CANTERBURY www.canterbury-cathedral.org
CARLISLE www.carlislecathedral.org.uk
CHELMSFORD www.chelmsfordcathedral.org.uk
CHESTER www.chestercathedral.com
CHICHESTER www.chichestercathedral.org.uk
COVENTRY www.coventrycathedral.org.uk

D

DERBY www.derbycathedral.org
DURHAM www.durhamcathedral.co.uk

E

ELY www.elycathedral.org
EXETER www.exeter-cathedral.org.uk

G

GLOUCESTER www.gloucestercathedral.org.uk
GUILDFORD www.guildfordcathedral.org

H

HEREFORD www.herefordcathedral.org

L

LEICESTER www.cathedral.leicester.anglican.org
LICHFIELD www.lichfield-cathedral.org
LINCOLN www.lincolncathedral.com
LIVERPOOL www.liverpoolcathedral.org.uk
LONDON, ST. PAUL'S www.stpauls.co.uk

M

  MANCHESTER   www.manchestercathedral.org

N

  NEWCASTLE   www.stnicholascathedral.co.uk

  NORWICH   www.cathedral.org.uk

O

  OXFORD, CHRISTCHURCH   www.chch.ox.ac.uk

P

  PETERBOROUGH   www.peterborough-cathedral.org.uk

  PORTSMOUTH   www.portsmouthcathedral.org.uk

R

  RIPON   www.riponcathedral.org.uk

  ROCHESTER   www.rochestercathedral.org

S

  ST. ALBANS   www.stalbanscathedral.org

  ST. EDMONDSBURY   www.stedscathedral.co.uk

  SALISBURY   www.salisburycathedral.org.uk

  SHEFFIELD   www.sheffieldcathedral.org

  SOUTHWARK   www.cathedral.southwark.anglican.org

  SOUTHWELL   www.southwellminster.org

T

  TRURO   www.trurocathedral.org.uk

W

  WAKEFIELD   www.wakefieldcathedral.org.uk

  WELLS   www. wellscathedral.org.uk

  WINCHESTER   www.winchester-cathedral.org.uk

  WORCESTER   www.worcestercathedral.co.uk

Y

  YORK   www.yorkminster.org